DATAFIL

Ocean

Trevor Day

Silver Dolphin

The author wishes to thank the following people and organizations for their assistance in the writing of this book:

Di Cooke, National Trainer and Assessor for the Royal Lifesaving Society, UK; Jonathan Tubb, British Museum; staff of the Submarine Museum, Gosport, Hampshire; trawler skipper Phil Scott; staff of Somerset Library Services; and staff of the National Oceanographic Library, Southampton and the British Library, London. The text includes the author's interpretations and does not necessarily reflect the opinion or policy of these people or organizations. The author's partner, Christina G.N. Day, for her insightful comments on the manuscript. The editorial and design team at Marshall Editions, London, who managed the project in such a friendly and attentive manner.

Published in the United States by
Silver Dolphin Books
An imprint of the Advantage Publishers Group
5880 Oberlin Drive, San Diego, CA 92121-4794
www.advantagebooksonline.com

A Marshall Edition
Conceived, edited and designed by
Marshall Editions Ltd
The Orangery
161 New Bond Street
London W1S 2UF
www.marshallpublishing.com

Copyright © Marshall Editions Developments Ltd, 2000

ISBN 1-57145-480-2
Library of Congress Cataloging-in-Publication Data available upon request.

Originated in Singapore by Master Image
Printed and bound in China by Excel Printing

1 2 3 4 5 00 01 02 03 04

Cover photography: front, tl Digital Vision, tr NGDC/NOAA, b Wolfgang Kaehler/Corbis; back, Overview: Images Colour Library, In Focus: David B. Fleetham/Oxford Scientific Films, FAQs: Digital Vision, Jobfile: Raymond Blythe/Oxford Scientific Films, Factfile: Digital Vision.

Contents

FAQs

FACTFILE

JOBFILE

How this book works

OVERVIEW

The colorful opening section introduces the amazing world of the oceans. A spectacular montage of images tells the story of ocean life, from its creatures to leisure activities, industry, transportation, and environmental issues. Alongside, a mini-essay looks at how vital the oceans are to all of us and how important it is that we maintain them.

FAQs

Packed full of fascinating facts, the FAQs—Frequently Asked Questions—file provides answers to some of the questions you've always wanted to ask. Why is the sea salty? What technology do scientists use to study the ocean? These are just some of the questions answered using simple diagrams and colorful photographs.

JOBFILE

Find out what it's like to work in a range of ocean industries, such as fishing and archaeology. There are interviews with people about their careers, including how they got started and what their job involves. Although the people are fictional, the work they describe is based on real life.

IN FOCUS

The essential information about oceans, their functions, and life is presented in this section, which is the largest in the *Datafile*. With the aid of photographs and diagrams, it looks at ocean geography and features, climate, ocean life, resources, navigation, new developments, and future possibilities.

FACTFILE

Providing ready reference at a glance, this file contains essential facts and figures in an easy-to-access format. It includes ocean facts and statistics, comparisons, a timeline, and a who's who. There's also a comprehensive illustrated glossary that explains technical terms used in the book.

OVERVIEW

Overview

The vital ocean

5–8

*"I do not know what I may appear to the world,
but to myself I seem to have been only like a boy playing
on the sea-shore, and diverting myself in now and then
finding a smoother pebble or a prettier shell
than ordinary, whilst the great ocean of truth
lay all undiscovered before me."*

Sir Isaac Newton (1642–1727)

I magine a world without oceans. Not so difficult, you might think. So, there would be no ocean fish, no seaweed, and no shellfish on the menu. There would be no trips to the beach to sunbathe and relax. No opportunities to swim or dive in the sea. No giant whales or dolphins. No coral reefs. No ocean cruises or recreational watersports like surfing and sailing. But much more than this, without the oceans there would probably be no life at all on our planet.

As far as we know, life evolved in the oceans. In the 1960s, when astronauts on Apollo space missions looked back at Earth, it was a cloud-streaked blue planet they saw: a planet of water, not a green-brown planet of land.

The oceans cover 71 percent of our planet. Nearly half of human population lives within 100 miles of the sea. Ninety-eight percent of the habitable part of the planet is in the oceans. On land, living space extends from treetops to deep caves, but even the deepest descend for only a few hundred yards. Most of the

"The oceans cover 71 percent of Earth"

world's ocean, however, is several miles deep. Creatures live in all parts of the ocean, from its sunlit surface to its darkest depths. The oceans are so vast that it is only in the last two hundred years that oceanography has begun in earnest. In the early 1900s, diving vehicles and hard-suited divers broke the 300-foot depth barrier. Up until

then, our knowledge of deep-ocean creatures was based largely on carcasses washed up on shore, on specimens caught in nets, and on dredges and seawater sample bottles. Today, we can explore the deepest ocean using robot vehicles, and scientists monitor vast areas of ocean surface using remote-sensing satellites.

Although fish and shellfish make up less than 10 percent of the world's diet, these foods are rich in high-quality protein, which is in short supply in many countries. Some communities depend upon sea produce for most of their protein.

Nowadays, most people travel abroad by plane rather than by ship, but the seas remain a vital highway for transportation. About 90 percent of heavy goods are transported by sea. Much of the world's food is also carried this way. And the world's navies—particularly their submarines and aircraft carriers—still help maintain peace across most of the world, by patrolling the oceans, above and below the surface.

We are damaging the oceans in numerous ways. Many of the pollutants we produce on land find their way into the oceans. Marine algae, the tiny plants floating in the sea's surface waters, produce about half of the world's oxygen. Killing marine algae with pollution is like cutting down tropical rainforests on land.

We are overfishing the seas. We are removing plant communities such as mangroves that grow at the sea edge and help stabilize shores.

"Global warming is changing ocean currents"

In 1997, a global survey called Reef Check estimated that more than 90 percent of the world's coral reefs had been visibly damaged by local activities such as tourism.

Global warming caused by air pollution is changing ocean currents in ways we cannot predict. Small changes in major surface currents massively affect the climate and weather on land. And if sea levels rise by 20 inches in the next hundred years, low-lying tropical islands such

as the Maldives, and many coastlines on the major continents, will be affected by flooding.

The value of the oceans to our overall quality of life is difficult to measure. How do we put a value on the rhythmic beat of ocean waves, a sun-drenched beach, or a crystal clear tropical lagoon?

What will the oceans be like in 20 years' time? The answer to this depends on people like you, the reader of this book. Each of us can make a difference. This book is a starting point to finding out more about the marvel, magic, and mystery of the oceans.

IN FOCUS

In Focus

Birth of the oceans

Water from rock • Meteorites and comets

The Earth is probably 4.6 billion years old. Sometime in Earth's early history, water filled the hollows on Earth's surface to form the oceans. Where did the water come from? Either it was present on the Earth already or it could have arrived from space. Or both these possibilities could be true...

Bubbling cauldron

The early Earth was blazing hot, and its surface was a sea of molten rock. The atmosphere was thick with water vapor released as steam from the rock. Slightly less than 4 billion years ago, the Earth began to cool, and its surface turned solid. Soon after, as the atmosphere cooled, the water vapor in the atmosphere turned to liquid. Clouds formed, and rain fell in a downpour that lasted thousands of years. As water filled hollows on the Earth's surface, so the oceans were born.

◁ **When the first oceans formed, lightning and erupting volcanoes punctuated the gloom of a downpour that lasted thousands of years.**

Dirty snowballs from space

Most scientists believe that not all of the oceans' water emerged from Earth's rocks. "Wet" rocks, flying through space as meteorites, would have struck the early Earth and added water to it. And comets, giant dirty snowballs that originate from the farthest reaches of the solar system, have been arriving since the Earth was young. They too would have struck the Earth's atmosphere, so adding their water to the oceans.

▷ **A comet is ice and rock debris left over from the birth of the solar system, traveling through space. When a comet approaches the Sun and partially melts, a tail of water vapor streaks the night sky.**

Blue planet

Earth's water • Water cycle

Extraterrestrials visiting our world for the first time might be puzzled as to why we call our planet Earth. From space, our planet looks blue, with over two-thirds of its surface covered in ocean. Planet Ocean would be a more accurate name for our world. As humans, we have a land-centered view of the planet because, for the most part, we live on solid ground.

▽ A false-color 3-D computer image of the ocean floor. The land is shown in brown. The four true oceans of the world—Atlantic, Arctic, Indian, and Pacific can be seen.

△◁ Oceans can be warm or cold depending on their location in the world. Tourists flock to tropical beaches where warm, clear blue waters lap the shore. The cold polar seas are dotted with icebergs.

Oceans

The ocean, made up of salty water, covers 71 percent of the planet. The continents divide this expanse of water into four separate oceans: the Pacific Ocean, the Atlantic Ocean, the Indian Ocean, and the Arctic Ocean. The Pacific Ocean is by far the largest. It contains about the same amount of water as the other three oceans combined. People talk of the Southern Ocean around Antarctica, but it is not a true ocean. It is an extension of the Pacific, Atlantic, and Indian oceans.

ARCTIC OCEAN

Eurasia

North America

ATLANTIC OCEAN

Africa

South America

PACIFIC OCEAN

Australia

INDIAN OCEAN

SOUTHERN OCEAN

Antarctica

Seas

"Sea" is another name we use for ocean. But "sea" also describes part of an ocean. For example, the Caribbean Sea is part of the Atlantic Ocean, and the Arabian Sea lies in the Indian Ocean. Some seas, such as the Mediterranean Sea and the Red Sea, are almost completely surrounded by land. They are connected to a nearby ocean by a narrow passage called a strait. "Gulf" is an alternative word for a sea, as in the Gulf of Mexico or Persian Gulf.

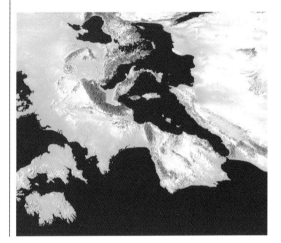

◁ **In this relief map of Europe, the Mediterranean Sea is seen from the west. The narrow Strait of Gibraltar at the bottom right of the picture connects the Mediterranean Sea to the Atlantic Ocean.**

Watery world

Most of the world's water (more than 97 percent) is found in the oceans. The amount of water in the ground (0.63 percent), in lakes and rivers (0.009 percent), and in the air (0.001 percent) is small, but it is vital to life on land. In the ocean or on land, water makes up more than two-thirds of the body of a plant or animal.

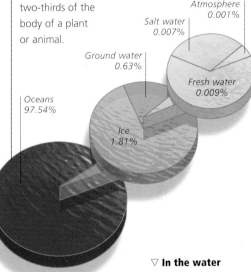

Atmosphere
0.001%

Salt water
0.007%

Ground water
0.63%

Fresh water
0.009%

Oceans
97.54%

Ice
1.81%

Moving water

Water on Earth is constantly on the move. Water from the surface of the oceans evaporates and enters the air, where it forms clouds. The clouds are blown across the ocean and return water to the sea when it rains, hails, or snows. Some clouds unload their water over land and so fill lakes and rivers and soak the ground. Soil and underground rocks take up plenty of water almost like a sponge. The water running off the land feeds streams, lakes, and rivers. Most of this water eventually returns to the sea at river estuaries.

▽ **In the water cycle water is circulated between sea, air, and land, as this diagram shows.**

Some clouds are blown over land or form over land

Clouds form

Rain, hail, and snow

Runoff from land

Flow below ground

Water evaporates from the ocean

Restless land and sea

Seafloor • Mid-ocean ridges
Ocean trenches • Earth's plates
Drifting continents • Changing oceans

The Earth's surface moves. Oceans and continents change shape. These movements happen over a timescale of many thousands of years. They shape the Earth's surface, creating the world's mountain peaks and the ocean depths.

Floating plates

The Earth's surface layer (crust) is made up of several large plates that float on a layer of semi-liquid rock (mantle). The plates move slowly, a few inches a year, powered by seafloor spreading. Where plates contain dense (heavy) rock, they have sunk to form depressions. Some of the larger depressions, called ocean basins, have filled with water to form oceans.

Ocean basin features

A typical mid-ocean ridge consists of a central rift valley (a sunken region of crust) flanked on either side by steep mountains. The existence of the Mid-Atlantic Ridge was confirmed in 1876 when mid-ocean depth readings were found to be much shallower than expected. Newspapers heralded the find as the discovery of the lost city of Atlantis.

New seafloor is made at mid-ocean ridges, where cracks in the ocean floor spew out magma, or molten rock. As the magma spreads away from the ridge, it cools, sinks, and buckles. In the process, the mid-ocean ridge comes to lie above a series of smaller features, called abyssal ridges, that form on each side.

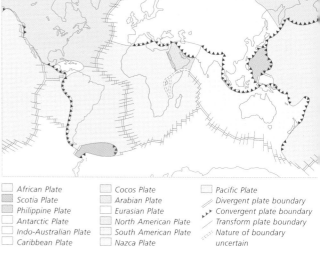

☐ African Plate	☐ Cocos Plate	☐ Pacific Plate
▩ Scotia Plate	☐ Arabian Plate	⟋ Divergent plate boundary
▨ Philippine Plate	☐ Eurasian Plate	⟋▸ Convergent plate boundary
☐ Antarctic Plate	☐ North American Plate	⟋ Transform plate boundary
☐ Indo-Australian Plate	☐ South American Plate	⟋ Nature of boundary
☐ Caribbean Plate	☐ Nazca Plate	uncertain

△ **The Earth's major plates support the oceans and continents. Movement of these plates causes continental drift.**

▽ **An ocean basin profile shows many different features.**

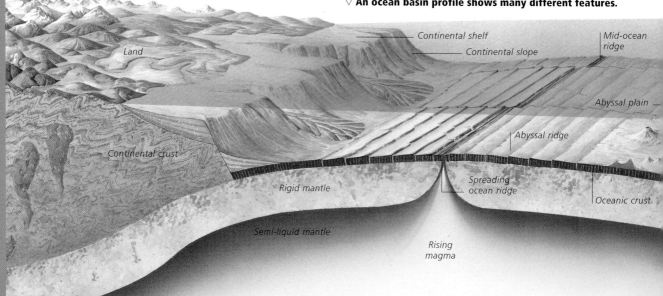

Continental shelf
Continental slope
Mid-ocean ridge
Land
Abyssal plain
Abyssal ridge
Continental crust
Rigid mantle
Spreading ocean ridge
Oceanic crust
Semi-liquid mantle
Rising magma

△ **Bodh Kharbu, a mountain in the Himalayas, was created about 35 million years ago when two continental plates collided.**

Where plates meet

The boundaries between plates are unstable regions of crust. Mid-ocean ridges develop where two adjacent plates move apart. A trench forms where one plate slides below another. At a fault line, two plates move past each other. They may catch and drag, causing earthquakes. Where two plates collide, one or both crumple to create jagged mountains.

▷ **At the San Andreas Fault near San Francisco, CA, two plates grind past each other and occasionally generate major earthquakes.**

Continental drift and shaping of oceans

As the plates move, they carry continents with them. About 250 million years ago, the Earth's surface supported just a single landmass, Pangaea. Over time, plate movements split Pangaea into fragments. These moved apart and occasionally crashed into one another to form the present-day continents separated by oceans, whose shape also changed in the process.

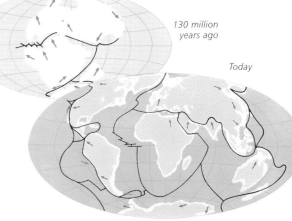

Pangaea *200 million years ago*

130 million years ago

Today

Down in the trenches

Seafloor is continually being created. The Earth's surface would grow unless some of it were removed at the same time. This happens at trenches. There, at subduction ("taking under") zones, old seafloor sinks below the Earth's crust and becomes part of the Earth's semi-liquid mantle again. Some of the molten rock finds its way back to the surface through nearby mountain-building volcanoes.

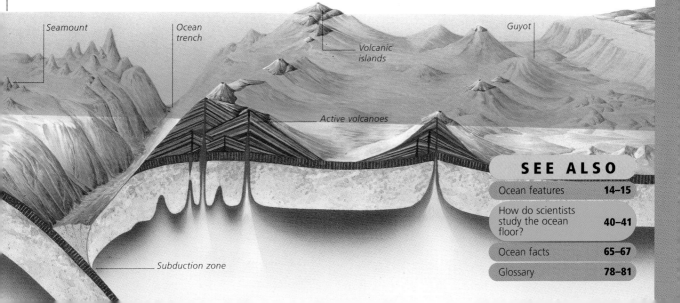

Seamount

Ocean trench

Volcanic islands

Active volcanoes

Guyot

Subduction zone

Ocean features

Continental margins • Submarine canyons
Oceanic islands • Seafloor sediments

If we could drain off the water from the oceans, we would reveal a landscape even more dramatic than that on land. On the ocean floor mountains are higher, valleys are deeper, and the plains extend for thousands of miles. The continuous movements of the Earth's plates and the process of seafloor spreading help create the physical features of the ocean floor.

Underwater avalanches

Parts of the continental shelf are scarred by deep canyons, called submarine canyons, some of which lie below river estuaries. Such canyons are slowly being eroded, widened, and deepened by water and sediment washing down the rivers. Other canyons are being carved by occasional underwater avalanches of water and sediment that sweep everything before them. These avalanches sometimes snap deep-sea cables.

▷ **Sediment carried down the submarine canyon gathers in a deep-sea fan. The fan spills from the continental rise onto the deep-ocean floor.**

Edges of continents

The continental margins are the submerged edges of continents. The continental shelf extends from the shore and is covered in seawater to an average depth of about 500 feet. At its outer edge, called the slope, the shelf drops away steeply to the deep-ocean floor beyond. Sediment settles on the slope and gathers at its base, the continental rise.

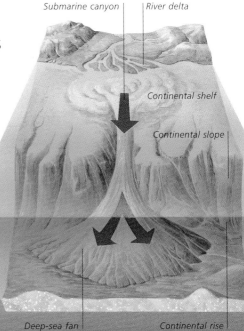

Submarine canyon | *River delta*

Continental shelf

Continental slope

Deep-sea fan | *Continental rise*

Terrigenous deposits

Calcareous deposits

Red clay

Radiolarian ooze

Diatom ooze

◁ **This map shows the distribution of the different kinds of sediments in the world's oceans.**

Rain of particles

A rain of small particles continuously falls to the ocean floor, forming a steadily thickening carpet. In the older parts of the ocean the sediment layer is 1,000–1,500 feet thick and has been forming over millions of years. There are several kinds of seabed deposit: terrigenous, from particles washed off the land; red clay, from dust blown out to sea; and calcareous, radiolarian, and diatom, from the sunken skeletons and shells of countless dead marine plankton.

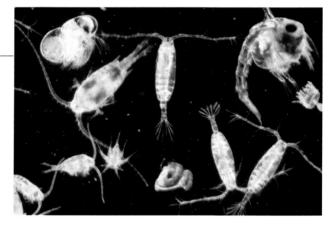

▷ **Marine plankton seen under a microscope. Some form seabed deposits when they die.**

Islands in the making

Hot spots are weaknesses in the Earth's crust. When an ocean plate passes over the hot spot, magma comes up through the seafloor, forming a volcano that travels thousands of feet toward the sea surface. If it breaks the surface, it forms a volcanic island; if it does not, it remains as an underwater mountain called a seamount. Some volcanic islands later sink to form seamounts. Guyots are seamounts with their tops flattened by erosion from rain, wind, and waves.

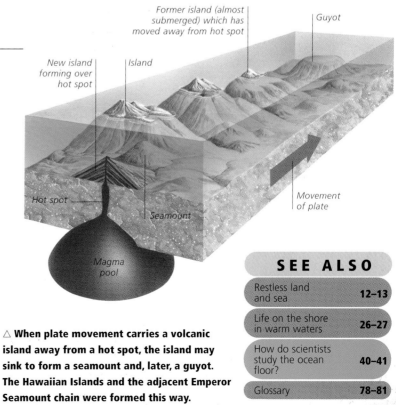

Former island (almost submerged) which has moved away from hot spot

Guyot

New island forming over hot spot

Island

Hot spot

Seamount

Magma pool

Movement of plate

◁ **The island of Surtsey, to the south of Iceland, was formed in 1963 by violent volcanic action below the Atlantic Ocean. Surtsey lies over the Mid-Atlantic Ridge. The plates in this area are slowly moving apart. The movement causes the occasional eruption.**

△ **When plate movement carries a volcanic island away from a hot spot, the island may sink to form a seamount and, later, a guyot. The Hawaiian Islands and the adjacent Emperor Seamount chain were formed this way.**

SEE ALSO

Restless land and sea	12–13
Life on the shore in warm waters	26–27
How do scientists study the ocean floor?	40–41
Glossary	78–81

Where land and sea meet

**Rocky shores • Sandy shores • Changing sea level
The shifting land • Global warming • Fighting the sea**

On coasts, the sea and land battle for victory. Along some parts of the coast, waves and currents gnaw away at hard rock to create cliffs. Elsewhere, where currents are slow, the sea sheds its load of particles onto sandy beaches or mud flats, and the land gradually extends seaward.

△ **A large pebble on a rocky beach has broken to reveal a fossil of an ammonite (an extinct mollusk).**

△ **Groynes help prevent sand from being swept away by waves and currents.**

The rise and fall of land and sea

When the world's climate changes, sea levels rise or fall. Only 12,000 years ago, at the end of the last ice age, the North Sea of Europe did not exist. In its place was land covered in ice. Since then, the ice has thawed, sea levels have risen by many feet, and seawater has flooded into the region to create the North Sea.
Over thousands and millions of years, sea levels not only rise and fall, but land is also pushed up or sinks down because of the continuous shifts in the Earth's crust. On the slopes of Mount Everest, the world's highest mountain, there is a band of shale formed from seafloor sediment. This shows that the mountain was once partially covered by seawater.

Sand and mud

The shore is the boundary between land and sea. It is regularly covered in seawater and then exposed to the air as tides rise and fall. Sandy shores and mud flats form on sheltered parts of the coastline. The stone particles eroded from rocky shores or emptied into the sea by rivers may travel many miles carried by coastal currents. Larger particles that are swept ashore settle to form sandy or pebbly beaches. Smaller particles travel farther and settle to form muddy shores in sheltered bays and estuaries.

▽ **A sandy beach is ideal for making sandcastles, but they will soon be swept away by the rising tide.**

▷ **The coastline at Etratet in Normandy, France, is the result of erosion by the sea. Rock stacks and arches are formed by the constant action of the waves against the cliffs.**

Wave attack

Dramatic rocky shores form where high land meets strong sea. The land is eroded, and cliffs, rock arches, and stacks may form. Below the cliffs, landslides may leave a tumble of rocks that will eventually create a wide wave-cut platform. This may contain pebbles and boulders, brought in by strong waves and powerful currents. The platform may grow to the extent that all but the largest waves are prevented from reaching the cliffs.

△ **Buildings collapse into the sea as the cliffs are eroded.**

A losing battle

The sea is immensely powerful. Although we can build sea defenses to prevent some of the sea's worst effects, we need to learn how to work with the sea's strength, rather than against it. In 1982, the citizens of Ocean City, New Jersey, paid $5 million to have an artificial sandy beach laid. The beach was swept away within three months.

Rising seas

The Earth's surface is getting warmer. An international group of scientists meeting in 1995 concluded that global sea levels would probably rise by about 20 inches in the next hundred years. This rise would be enough to cover important low-lying coastal areas scattered throughout the world. Measures, such as building flood defenses, can be taken to protect some of these areas.

△ **If sea levels rise by 20 in. as the oceans get warmer, some of the low-lying Maldive Islands in the Indian Ocean will disappear under the sea.**

△ **Ebb tide at Mont St. Michel.**

△ **Flood tide at Mont St. Michel.**

Tides and waves

Tides • Gravitational pull and its effect
Tidal currents, surges, and bores
Waves • The action of waves

The relentless action of tides and waves erodes the shoreline in some places and deposits sediment in others. Tides and waves are major forces in the lives of animals and plants that live on the shore and in the surface waters of the sea.

Tidal movements

The tide is a regular rise and fall in sea level over several hours. It is caused by the gravitational attraction of the Moon and, to a lesser extent, the Sun. As the Moon orbits the Earth, it pulls the Earth's water toward it, creating a bulge. This would cause the spinning Earth to become lopsided and start to wobble, but a balancing bulge of water develops on Earth's opposite side. Where bulges form, it is high tide. In between, where water has been withdrawn, it is low tide.

The Earth spins on its axis once every 24 hours, so most coasts experience two tidal bulges in a day. However, as tidal bulges move across the Earth, they are deflected and blocked by landmasses and underwater obstructions, so complicating the simple pattern. The Gulf of Mexico, for example, has only one tide a day instead of two.

Spring and neap tides

About twice a month, the Moon and Sun are in alignment, and their gravitational pulls reinforce each other. As a result, the high tide is much higher than normal and the low tide much lower. These are the spring tides. They occur at the full moon and the new moon. Halfway between these times, the Sun and Moon pull at right angles, and their gravitational effects work against each other to produce a smaller tidal bulge. The tidal range (the difference between high and low tides) becomes much smaller. These are the neap tides.

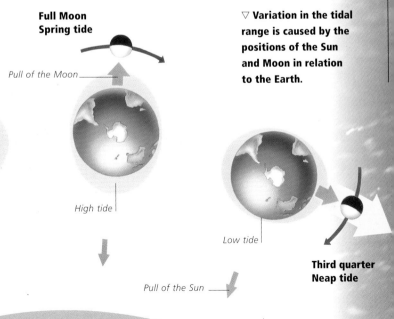

Full Moon
Spring tide

Pull of the Moon

▽ **Variation in the tidal range is caused by the positions of the Sun and Moon in relation to the Earth.**

Earth

First quarter
Neap tide

High tide

Low tide

Moon

Third quarter
Neap tide

New Moon
Spring tide

Pull of the Sun

Sun

The strength and energy behind the tide

As tidal bulges move along coasts and pass through narrow channels, they can produce dangerous tidal currents with speeds of more than 10 miles an hour. When a tidal bulge reaches shallow water, the water piles up and surges forward. During a high spring tide, the surge may funnel into an estuary to form a wall of water that rushes upstream. This is a tidal bore. The biggest bores happen on the Chientang River in China, where they reach over 23 feet in height.

◁ **Riding the surf of a tidal bore in a dinghy has become a popular and exciting pastime. The bigger the bore, the more exhilarating the ride.**

△ **Mussels are shore animals that are alternately submerged and uncovered as the tide rises and falls.**

Wind motion

Most waves are generated by winds. The bigger the wind and the longer it blows, the larger the wave it creates. Out at sea, a wave is an up and down movement that travels across the sea surface. The particles in a wave tend to stay where they are and move in circles, rather than being carried along by the wave. When a wave reaches shallow water, the wave breaks and its crest topples forward, crashing to form surf. Any small particles in the wave are now pushed up the beach.

▷ **The water in a wave goes up and down in a circle in the same place. Waves break in shallow water to become surf.**

▷ **The best waves for surfing are found on gently sloping beaches, where waves break gradually and surfers can "ride the tube."**

Wave power

At sea, the up and down movement of waves mixes the water in the top few yards and helps distribute oxygen and nutrients to the organisms that live there. On sandy shores, waves that strike the coastline at an angle shift sand and pebbles along the shore. On rocky shores, storm waves erode the base of cliffs. The very biggest waves are created by storms, volcanoes, and earthquakes. These giant waves wreck ships and can devastate towns and cities near coasts.

Oceans, currents, and climate

**Winds across the world • From winds come currents
The life-giving ocean • In the doldrums • Trade winds
and ocean currents • The Gulf Stream • Cloud seeders**

The oceans are massive shifting stores of heat and
moisture. They have an enormous influence on the
local, short-term changes in the atmosphere that we call
weather and on the more widespread, longer-term changes
we call climate. Wherever we live, whether we are
experiencing rain or sun, wind or calm, the oceans
have played their part.

Earth's major wind systems

The Earth's poles are much
cooler than the equator.
This temperature difference
between the equator and
the poles powers the world's
major winds. As warm air
rises from the equator, it
is replaced by cooler air from
the poles. This generates
wind circulations, or cells, at
different latitudes. The Earth
spinning on its axis deflects
these winds along recognizable
paths, creating the Earth's
major wind systems.

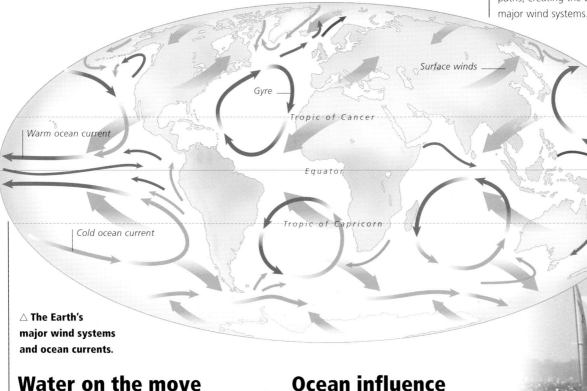

Gyre

Surface winds

Tropic of Cancer

Warm ocean current

Equator

Cold ocean current

Tropic of Capricorn

△ **The Earth's
major wind systems
and ocean currents.**

Water on the move

Winds blowing across the surface of the sea drag
some of the water with them and so create currents.
Like winds, water currents are deflected (change
direction) by the spin of the Earth. Giant spiral patterns
of water movement called gyres are generated in this
way. Gyres turn clockwise in the northern hemisphere
and counterclockwise in the southern hemisphere.

Ocean influence

The movement of water from the tropics
to the poles and back again spreads heat
throughout the world. Without oceans,
the tropics would be much hotter and the
poles much cooler. Since oceans heat up
and cool down more slowly than the land,
they influence the climate of coastal areas.

Land and sea breezes

On a sunny day, the land warms up more quickly than the sea. As the warm air rises, it draws in the cooler sea air, creating a sea breeze. At night, the sea cools more slowly than the land, so the air flows from land to sea, creating a land breeze.

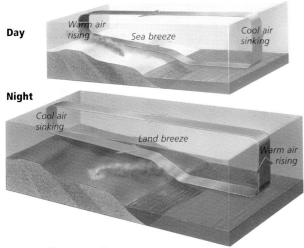

Figure eight

For seafarers in historical times, lack of knowledge of winds and currents could add weeks or months to a voyage. Portuguese seafarers of the 15th century discovered that it was quicker and easier to follow a figure eight path when sailing from Europe to South Africa and back again. This route followed the trade winds (winds blowing toward the equator) and the major ocean currents.

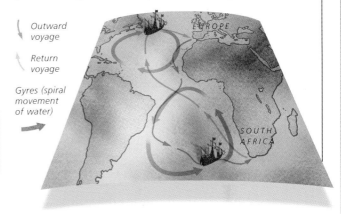

Outward voyage

Return voyage

Gyres (spiral movement of water)

Follow the Stream

Famous American statesman and inventor Benjamin Franklin was the first person to plot the route of the Gulf Stream, the warm ocean current that flows northeastward from the Gulf of Mexico toward northwestern Europe. Atlantic seafarers were able to shorten their journeys by riding on the Gulf Stream from America to Britain, and by avoiding it on their return.

▽ **With their sails billowing, these boats use the full potential of the wind to carry them across the sea.**

Chemical clouds

Phytoplankton (microscopic plants) seed clouds so they may influence our weather and climate. Some release a chemical, DMS for short, that rises into the air and causes water to condense (change from gas to liquid). This triggers cloud formation. Creating clouds could have several advantages for the phytoplankton: it may shield them from dangerous ultraviolet rays; rain may wash nutrients out of the air; and updrafts may even help carry phytoplankton through the air and disperse them.

Phytoplankton, plants that live in water

Ocean life

Light, temperature, and pressure
The zones • Food chains

Scientists describe the underwater world of the oceans by dividing it into different depth zones. The zones differ in their physical conditions, particularly their light level, temperature, and water pressure. Each zone supports a different community of organisms, specially adapted to that environment.

Ocean zone environments

In the clearest oceans, sunlight only penetrates to a depth of 3,000 feet, and most is absorbed in the first 650 feet. The presence or absence of light determines the nature and numbers of ocean creatures in the different zones. Water temperature drops with depth. In the very deep ocean, water pressure is one thousand times greater than at the surface.

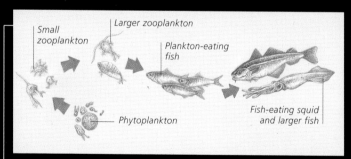

△ **Phytoplankton, which are at the start of the food chain, are consumed by zooplankton. These are eaten by larger zooplankton and small fish. Top predators include larger fish.**

Sea food

Ocean creatures depend on plants, directly or indirectly, for their survival. Tiny plants called phytoplankton trap sunlight to make their own food. They are eaten by small animal plankton (zooplankton) which, in turn, are eaten by larger zooplankton. Small fish strain seawater with their gills to extract plankton. Larger predators feed on the smaller fish. Deep-sea creatures feed on the remains of dead plants and animals that fall to the ocean floor.

The sunlit zone

This zone extends to a depth of 650 feet. Here there is enough sunlight to fuel the growth of green plants. Drifting microscopic algae, or phytoplankton, are numerous and are eaten by many other organisms. The plants of the sunlit zone—directly or indirectly—provide the food for almost all the animals of the open ocean.

The twilight zone

Dim sunlight penetrates to this level, but not enough to sustain the growth of plants. In the strange half-light, many fish and squid generate their own light (bioluminescence). Their skin pattern of dark and light breaks up their outline, making them less visible to predators. Many inhabitants of the twilight zone rise to the surface waters at night to feed on phytoplankton.

The dark zone

In the cold dark waters of this zone there is no sunlight at all. The creatures that inhabit the dark zone are often nightmarish—with huge mouths and small bodies—but on a miniature scale. Most of the fish are much less than 3 feet long. There is little food at this depth, and fish cannot afford to let any prey escape, hence their big jaws and long, sharp teeth.

The abyss

In this high pressure environment, which is colder than the dark zone, food is even more sparse. Creatures living here tend to gather on or just above the seafloor, waiting to feed on waste matter or the occasional dead animal that drifts down. On the deep-ocean floor, the community of fish, crabs, shrimp, and shrimplike creatures called amphipods will strip a carcass to the bone within hours.

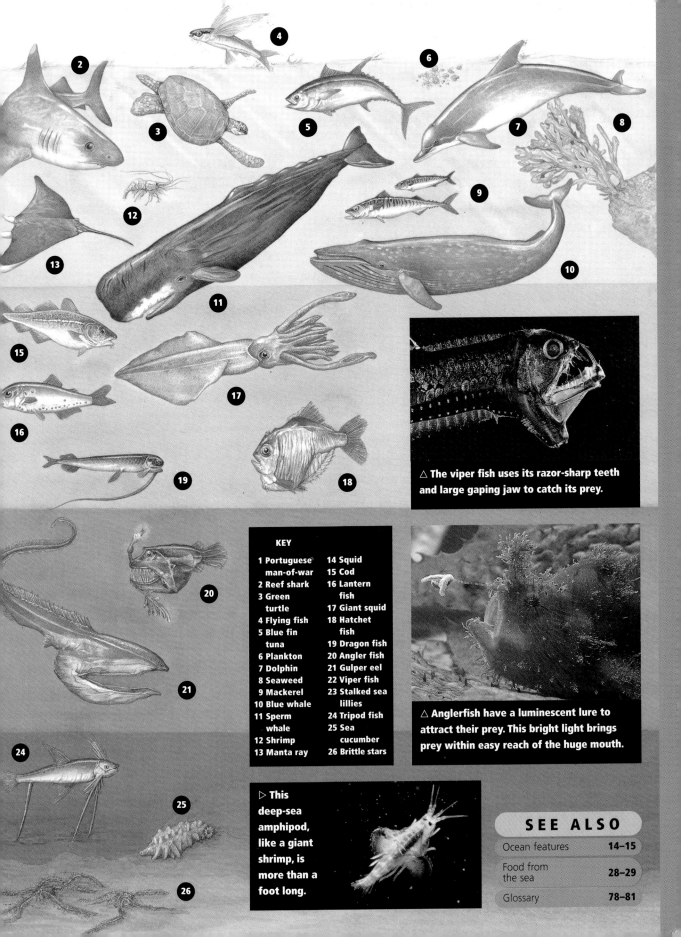

△ The viper fish uses its razor-sharp teeth and large gaping jaw to catch its prey.

△ Anglerfish have a luminescent lure to attract their prey. This bright light brings prey within easy reach of the huge mouth.

▷ This deep-sea amphipod, like a giant shrimp, is more than a foot long.

KEY

1 Portuguese man-of-war
2 Reef shark
3 Green turtle
4 Flying fish
5 Blue fin tuna
6 Plankton
7 Dolphin
8 Seaweed
9 Mackerel
10 Blue whale
11 Sperm whale
12 Shrimp
13 Manta ray
14 Squid
15 Cod
16 Lantern fish
17 Giant squid
18 Hatchet fish
19 Dragon fish
20 Angler fish
21 Gulper eel
22 Viper fish
23 Stalked sea lillies
24 Tripod fish
25 Sea cucumber
26 Brittle stars

Life on the shore in cool waters

Rocky shores • Sandy shores • Estuaries
Kelp forests • Seagrass meadows

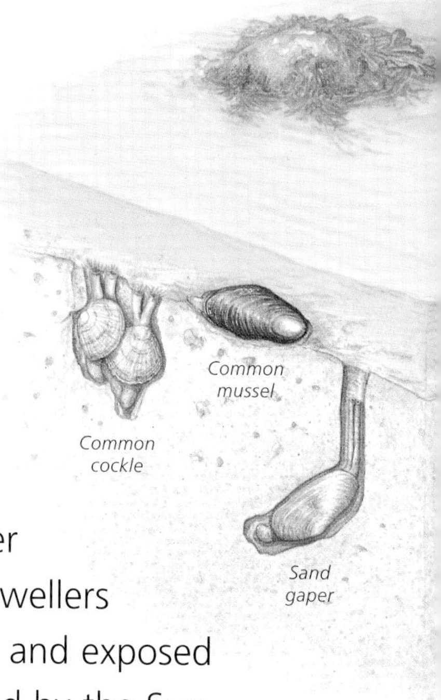

Common mussel
Common cockle
Sand gaper

The shore—where land and sea meet—is a difficult environment for animals and plants to live in. Water levels rise and fall with the tides, and these shore dwellers find themselves alternately covered in seawater and exposed to the air. They must cope with being baked by the Sun and, a few hours later, being battered by the waves.

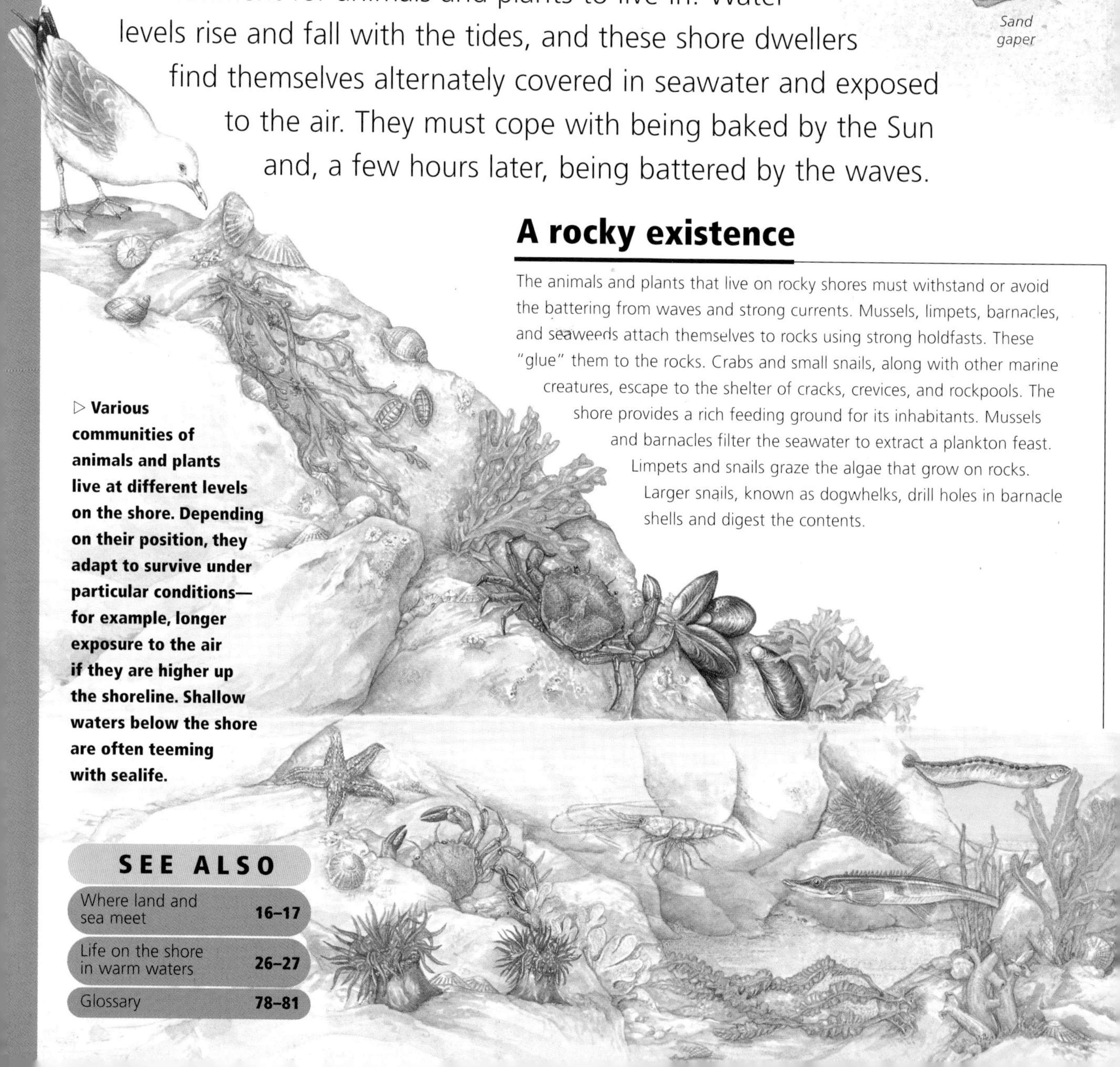

A rocky existence

The animals and plants that live on rocky shores must withstand or avoid the battering from waves and strong currents. Mussels, limpets, barnacles, and seaweeds attach themselves to rocks using strong holdfasts. These "glue" them to the rocks. Crabs and small snails, along with other marine creatures, escape to the shelter of cracks, crevices, and rockpools. The shore provides a rich feeding ground for its inhabitants. Mussels and barnacles filter the seawater to extract a plankton feast. Limpets and snails graze the algae that grow on rocks. Larger snails, known as dogwhelks, drill holes in barnacle shells and digest the contents.

▷ Various communities of animals and plants live at different levels on the shore. Depending on their position, they adapt to survive under particular conditions—for example, longer exposure to the air if they are higher up the shoreline. Shallow waters below the shore are often teeming with sealife.

SEE ALSO

Where land and sea meet	**16–17**
Life on the shore in warm waters	**26–27**
Glossary	**78–81**

Lugworm

Thin tellin

Razorshell

Spider crab

△ **To survive on a sandy shore, animals live below the sand.**

Forests in the sea

In some cool, shallow waters, where the sea bottom is rocky, huge seaweeds called kelp grow in abundance. Their fronds, like giant leaves, reach many yards in length. They create a dense underwater forest that extends from the seafloor to the surface. Kelp can grow very quickly, as much as 20 inches a day. A community of tiny plants and animals grows on the kelp. Lobsters, crabs, worms, sea stars, and fish hunt, graze, and forage in and around the kelp forest and are themselves the prey of seals and sea otters.

△ **A common seal swims through a dense kelp forest.**

Underwater meadows

Seagrasses are descended from land plants. They grow in shallow water where the sea bottom is soft. Seagrasses have flowers, which open underwater. Pollen is carried from one flower to another on water currents. Seagrass meadows harbor many creatures and serve as natural barriers that protect coastlines from erosion by waves and currents. Endangered animals, such as turtles, dugongs, and manatees, are among the few animals that eat seagrasses.

Beach life

The surface of a sandy shore may look inviting to us, but it is a hostile environment for small creatures. They cannot grip the sand particles to stop themselves from being washed away. However, many holes and worm casts show that there are countless burrowing animals living below the surface. When tidal waters rise and cover the sand, many of the creatures extend their legs, tentacles, or siphons into the water to feed. They filter the water for plankton or scratch at the sandy surface, seeking food.

△ **Flocks of wading seabirds feed in the shallow waters of a salt marsh.**
▷ **The common oystercatcher probes for deep-burrowing animals using its long bill.**

River's end

An estuary is the place where a river joins the sea. Fine sediment settles in and around estuaries to form mud flats. Burrowing animals live in the mud. As oxygen can only penetrate the top layers of tightly packed mud particles, many animals live just below the surface mud. Others create water currents in their burrows to draw in oxygen-rich water. Estuaries are important parts of the marine environment. The early life stages of many fish, mollusks, and crustaceans grow there, and exposed mud flats support large populations of wading seabirds.

▽ **A seagrass meadow grows in shallow waters.**

Life on the shore in warm waters

▽ Fish swim through a colorful soft coral garden.

Coral polyps • Coral reefs
Coral reef communities • Mangrove swamps

The clear shallows of tropical and subtropical seas are home to the most luxuriant communities in the ocean— coral reefs. They are the marine equivalent of tropical rainforests on land. Mangrove trees often grow on shores nearby. Their roots and branches straddle the boundary between land, sea, and air.

Mouth

Tentacle

◁ It takes thousands of these coral polyps to make a clump of coral.

Rocky skeleton

A strange partnership

Coral reefs may grow many miles long and yet they are created by tiny organisms, called hard coral polyps, most of which are less than 10 millimeters across. Each polyp creates a hard protective skeleton of limestone around itself. The polyp feeds on tiny plankton using its tentacles. It also harbors welcome guests called zooxanthellae—special algae that live within its body. The algae trap sunlight and manufacture food. The polyp, in return, provides a safe home.

How coral reefs form

When hard coral polyps die, their chalky cases remain behind. New polyps settle on top, so the reef grows. The polyps only grow in warm, sun-drenched seawater. Under these conditions, fringing reefs form in shallow water along coasts. If the nearby land sinks, the reef continues to grow offshore, forming a barrier reef. When a fringing reef develops around a volcanic island, and the island sinks, a circular barrier reef forms. If the island then sinks completely, a ring of coral—a coral atoll—remains.

Coral atoll

Barrier reef

Fringing reef

△ The diagram shows how the three main types of coral reef form.

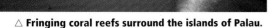

△ Fringing coral reefs surround the islands of Palau.

Every nook and cranny

There are hundreds of different kinds of coral. They grow in many colors and shapes—to look like ferns, deer antlers, mushrooms, and even human brains—and create an intricate patchwork in the sea, where plants and animals can settle or hide. Only a few animals feed directly on the coral. Many more graze on the film of algae that grows on the coral, eat the plankton that drifts past, or hunt larger creatures.

Moorish idol

◁ **A pink anemonefish is immune to the stinging tentacles of its host anemone.**

Lionfish

A multicolored world

Many of the reef's inhabitants are vividly colored. In many cases, the bright colors and bold patterns advertise that the animal is unpleasant to eat or is actually poisonous. Lionfish, for example, carry venomous spines. In some cases, bold patterns enable members of the same species to recognize each other on the crowded reef. In other instances, the stripes and patterns serve to break up the body outline and so provide camouflage.

Reaching for the sky

Mangrove trees grow on muddy tropical and subtropical shores. Most mangroves have roots that rise above the mud. They help support the tree and absorb oxygen from the air. Frogs, snakes, bats, and birds live in the branches. These animals feed on each other, on insects, and on animal life in the water below. Algae and small animals grow attached to the submerged roots. Fish and crustaceans enter and leave the area with the tide, and the mud contains many worms and shellfish. Mangrove swamps are important nursery areas for young fish and shellfish.

◁ **Mangrove trees, with their exposed roots, flourish in the warm waters of tropical shores.**

SEE ALSO

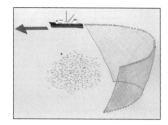

Food from the sea

Fishing • Hunting • Farming the seas

Fish and other seafood are an invaluable source of protein, but as we have continued to catch more, the seas have become seriously overfished. Many of the ocean's major fish populations have decreased in numbers. In the 1990s, the total amount of seafood taken each year was 80–85 million tons. Growing fish in fish farms is becoming increasingly necessary to make good the shortfall in fish being caught at sea.

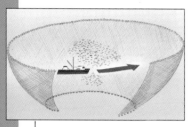

△ **A purse seine net is used to catch open-water fish. The net encircles the fish and is closed off at the bottom to trap them. It is then pulled up to the surface.**

▽ **A fishing trawler uses a purse seine net to haul in its catch. Such nets are used to catch tuna, anchovies, and sardines.**

Fish trade

More than half of the world's fish are caught in shallow waters on continental shelves, using large nets. Fishermen gut and freeze larger fish soon after capture and later sell them as food for people. Smaller fish, such as anchovies and sardines, when not being used for human consumption, are often ground up and used as animal feed, fertilizer, and in products such as glue, soap, and paint.

Mackerel

Anchovy

Skipjack tuna

▽ **Drift nets may be several miles long. They accidentally catch endangered sea creatures and so are banned in most waters.**

Surface fishing

Sardine

Pelagic fish are those that live near the surface of the ocean or in midwater. They include anchovies, sardines, herring, mackerel, and tuna. One technique used to catch this type of fish is the large purse seine net, which can trap a whole school. Larger pelagic fish can also be caught using longlines baited with hooks. Another net fishermen use is the gill net, which is set vertically in the water. Fish swim into the net and become entangled or ensnared by their gills. Drift nets are enormously long floating gill nets. Unfortunately, dolphins and turtles can get trapped in them as well as the intended fish.

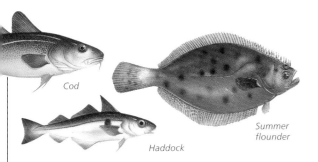

Cod

Haddock

Summer flounder

> A trawl net is like an open bag of netting. It is pulled along by a trawler and catches fish living on or near the seafloor.

School of fish

Floats, weights, and boards keep the mouth of the net open

Bottom fishing

Demersal, or bottom-living, fish include cod, haddock, pollock, and flatfish such as flounder, plaice, sole, and turbot. They are caught with trawl nets, which look rather like giant bags. The net is dragged along the seabed or just above it. Trawl nets are also used to catch shellfish such as crabs and scallops. Unfortunately, unwanted fish and other creatures are caught along with the valuable fish, and this by-catch is often dumped at sea. Many demersal fish are gutted and frozen at sea on large factory ships.

Fish farms

The Chinese have been farming fish, shellfish, and seaweed for at least four thousand years. In western countries, farming sea creatures is a more recent activity. Today, about one quarter of the money we spend on fish and shellfish is spent on farmed creatures. In China, milkfish are reared in shallow coastal ponds. In many parts of the world, clams, mussels, and oysters are grown in baskets, or on ropes, wooden frames, or fences in shallow water. From Norway to Chile, salmon are grown in floating cages in the sea or in tanks on land. As the seas become increasingly overfished, farming the sea is likely to become even more important.

▽ Pens or tanks are used to hold the fish at a fish farm. Scientists monitor the health and growth of the fish.

A cruel practice

Nowadays, relatively few large sea creatures are hunted for food. Some traditional peoples catch whales, seals, and other sea mammals on a restricted basis. Young and adult fur seals are taken in northern Canada; Faroe Islanders catch pilot whales; and in parts of Asia dolphins are hunted. Between the 1600s and 1980s, many of the world's populations of large whales dropped to less than 10 percent of their original numbers as a result of hunting. Today there is a moratorium (a temporary ban) on the hunting of larger whales. Most countries abide by this.

◁ A dead sperm whale is dragged ashore for processing.

Energy and minerals from the sea

How oil and gas form • Sand and gravel
Salt • Valuable metals • Metals in the deep sea

For thousands of years, the seas have been a generous provider of common salt and building materials such as sand and gravel. Within the last 150 years, prospectors have found ways to drill and mine beneath the seas. The seabed, and the rocks below it, now yield valuable metals, oil, and natural gas.

From sea creatures to oil and gas

Petroleum oil and natural gas sometimes form below shallow seas. This happens when sea creatures are buried rapidly but decay slowly. Over many thousands of years, heat and pressure deep underground transform the remains into oil and gas. Special conditions are needed for the oil and gas to gather in large deposits that can be reached by prospectors. The substances must be trapped in porous (penetrable) layers below impermeable (impenetrable) rock.

Impermeable rock blocks off the escape of oil and gas

Oil and gas gather in porous rock

Oil passes up through a layer of porous rock

Mining seashores

The value of sand and gravel mined offshore is second only to that of oil and gas. Beaches and riverbeds from the most recent ice ages, now covered in water, contain large deposits of sand and gravel (called aggregates) which can be extracted. Geologists have realized that mining seashores for their sand damages the coastline and encourages erosion. Increasingly, therefore, sand and gravel are dredged from shallow waters offshore. In industry, these aggregates are used in making concrete and other building materials. Sand is also used in glassmaking.

▷ **Men in Assam, India, extract sand from shallow coastal waters.**

Salty waters

Common salt, or sodium chloride, is—apart from water itself—the most abundant substance in seawater. On average there is about 1 ounce of salt and other dissolved solids in every quart of seawater. We need some salt in our diet. The salt added to food is a preservative, and it enhances flavor. It can replace the salt we lose when we sweat. In ancient Rome, people were sometimes paid in salt as part of their wages—the word "salary" comes from the Latin for salt.

◁ **Piles of sea salt in Sicily, Italy—where the climate is warm—are collected by allowing seawater to dry out in ponds or lagoons.**

Deep-sea riches

Potato-sized lumps of rock, rich in metals, are scattered over much of the deep sea. These lumps, called manganese nodules, form naturally and are a source of manganese, copper, and nickel. In some parts of the ocean, volcanic activity causes superheated water, rich in valuable metals, to spew out through chimneys called hydrothermal vents. The metals settle around the vents.

▷ **Manganese nodules lie on the seafloor in the central North Pacific, at a depth of 19,260 feet. Scientists are trying to devise ways to harvest these metals.**

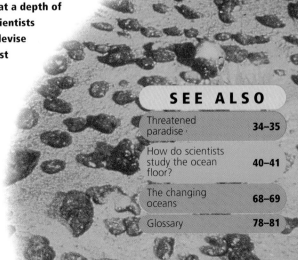

Precious resources

There is enough gold suspended in the oceans to make each person on Earth a solid gold ball weighing nearly 9 pounds. However, the precious metal is too spread out to be worth extracting. Mining is only worthwhile if metals are concentrated in large amounts. Tin and chromium are mined from shallow water where they have been eroded from the land and deposited on the seafloor. Waves and currents sort the metals by weight and size, and drop them in bands near the shore.

Modern navigation

Radar • Sonar • Lighthouses
Global positioning system (GPS)

▽ **On the bridge of a modern ferry, an electronic chart plotter displays the ship's position. The plotter system can be programmed to steer the vessel automatically on a planned course once it has left harbor.**

In the past, seafarers navigated by the Sun and stars and plotted their progress on wooden or paper charts. They smelled the air and tasted the seawater to help decide exactly where they were. Nowadays, seafarers using the latest technology can pinpoint their position to within a few meters at the touch of a button.

Radio detection

Radar (**RA**dio **D**etection **A**nd **R**anging) was developed during World War II. Nowadays, ships carry radar scanners that display nearby coasts and islands and reveal the position of vessels in the area. In busy seaways such as the English Channel, radar stations ashore monitor the movement of shipping and radio instructions to vessels. The use of radar has massively reduced the likelihood of collisions.

△ **Modern navigational instruments often have computer-generated visual displays.**

▷ **Whether people are sailing for pleasure or work, electronic navigation systems help, but good seamanship still relies upon the ability to plot a chart and use guides such as marker buoys, ships' lights, and lighthouses.**

Pulses of sound

Sonar (**SO**und **N**avigation **A**nd **R**anging) was originally developed during World War I to enable ships to detect submarines and avoid other underwater dangers. In traditional sonar, pulses of sound are transmitted downward through the water, and as they bounce off objects, their reflections are picked up by a detector. The size and distance of the object is displayed on screen.

Emitted sound waves

Reflected sound waves forming "echo"

◁ **A ship's sonar system reveals the depth of the seafloor and can detect underwater vessels such as submarines and other objects. Modern sonar can even detect schools of fish.**

△ **A lighthouse is a beacon in the night for seafarers.**

Beacon in the night

Lighthouses are among the oldest navigation aids. The Pharos lighthouse of Alexandria, Egypt—one of the seven wonders of the ancient world—was completed in 283 B.C. Modern lighthouses, like ancient ones, provide a reliable marker point and warn of possible hazards such as submerged rocks. The flashing light can be seen at distances of 20 miles or more. Each lighthouse's combination of height, shape, color, and flash rate is unique. By night and day, sailors take bearings (measure direction) from lighthouses and other reliable markers to figure out their position.

◁ **Good navigators use traditional methods as well as electronic ones such as this handheld GPS, as a check and as backup in case of system failure.**

Satellites

Overhead, 24 global positioning system (GPS) satellites travel on fixed orbits around the Earth. Each transmits time and identification signals that are detected by computerized GPS equipment on board ships. From any point on Earth, a ship receives a stream of data from four or more satellites, which the ship's GPS computer uses to calculate the vessel's position to within a few tens of yards.

SEE ALSO

How do scientists study the ocean floor? 40–41

How do fishermen find fish? 44–45

Timeline of surface exploration 72–73

Glossary 78–81

Threatened paradise

Mangrove swamps • Trawling and dredging
Oceanic islands • Pollution • Coral reefs

The world's oceans are under attack: from fishermen who are chasing fewer and fewer fish; from developers seeking shorelines on which to build; from tourists who damage coral reefs or buy souvenirs made from endangered sea creatures; and from all of us who pollute the seas—whether or not we are aware of it.

Thriving communities

Shorelines where mangroves grow may harbor fewer species than many other marine environments, but they are nursery grounds for many commercially important fish and shellfish. Native peoples have lived in harmony with mangrove communities for thousands of years, using the wood for building materials and fuel, and harvesting the plants and animals that live above and below the waterline. In the last few hundred years, about half of the world's coastal mangroves have been removed to accommodate farms, fish or shellfish farming, and coastal towns and cities. The removal of mangroves often makes the coastline more liable to flooding and erosion.

Damage to the seabed

Trawling for fish and shellfish can leave a path of destruction in its wake. The seafloor may be swept clean of almost all larger life forms. Many burrowing worms and shellfish are killed or their lives are disrupted. Sediments stirred up from the seafloor smother organisms. Only recently have scientists begun to appreciate the long-term damage that trawling and dredging can cause.

◁ **Dredging operations in Singapore harbor continue to remove or smother the local seabed. Mangroves have been removed to create this heavily developed coastline.**

Castaway

Islands far from land support unique communities of organisms that have evolved there. These islands are also very attractive to tourists. Such islands are very susceptible to damage— whether by accident or not. Some of the animal and plant communities of the Galápagos Islands, made famous by Charles Darwin, have been devastated by the introduction of goats and rats.

△ **If left untreated, this loon covered in spilt oil will soon die of starvation and heat loss.**

◁ **These exotic shells and coral skeletons were once homes to living creatures. Corals take years to regrow.**

▽ **An environmental disaster is caused as oil spills into the sea from the damaged tanker, the *Erika*.**

Poisoning the seas

We become most aware of sea pollution when we hear news reports of a tanker running aground and spilling oil. However, most marine pollution is happening all the time. Sewers discharge human waste into the sea, chimneys belch chemicals that will enter the oceans when it rains, and industries release chemicals into rivers that eventually flow into the sea. Worldwide, fishermen discard or lose more than 100,000 tons of fishing line and netting each year. Atmospheric pollution may be adding to the greenhouse effect and causing global warming. Changes in ocean currents caused by global warming are likely to have a great impact on life on land as well as in the sea.

▷ **This Antarctic fur seal is entangled in nylon net.**

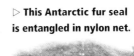

▽ **Coral is killed by objects dropping on it or if it is smothered with sediment.**

Reef damage

Coral reefs are sensitive to being smothered with silt or poisoned by pollution. Many reefs are overfished, or clumps of coral are removed to provide souvenirs. Sometimes reefs are poisoned with cyanide to stun fish so they can be taken for the aquarium trade. Tourists damage reefs when they accidentally kick or touch the fragile coral or lower a boat's anchor onto it. In 1997, a worldwide survey called Reef Check calculated that about 90 percent of the world's coral reefs showed visible signs of recent damage.

Making use of the sea

Underwater homes • Artificial islands • Leisure pursuits Sea travel • Navies

We do not often think of the importance oceans have in our daily lives. Many of the goods we buy have been shipped across seas. In times of war, attacks are often launched from the sea. Coastal land—whether as living space or for leisure—is highly desirable. With space on land under pressure, and the ocean world so attractive, living on or under the sea is increasingly likely in the future.

At home under the sea

In the future, properties will be built that extend below the sea surface as well as above. It may become possible to use solar energy to generate underwater electrical currents. These could remove chemicals from the sea and deposit them on frameworks to form artificial concretelike structures rather like the skeletons of hard corals, but on a larger scale. A building could be grown this way from the seafloor up.

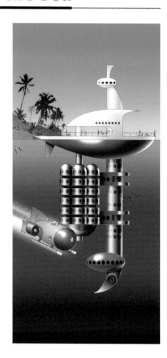

▷ **Perhaps the underwater hotels of the future will look something like this, with fantastic "ocean" views from all the rooms.**

At home on the sea

Seafront land is among the most sought after. In Tokyo, several artificial offshore islands have been built in response to the city's housing problem and the demand for office space. In 20 years' time, the world's highest-value properties may be built on artificial islands that could be towed from one place to another to take advantage of the changing seasons.

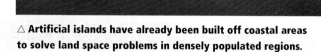

△ **Artificial islands have already been built off coastal areas to solve land space problems in densely populated regions.**

Enjoying the sea

The hypnotic ebb and flow of water on a sandy beach has always had a magical attraction. Within the last ten years, we have discovered many more ways of enjoying the natural beauty of the sea, whether through diving or snorkeling, as a passenger in a semisubmersible, or on a whale-watching excursion. Boating and sport fishing remain popular on coasts throughout the world.

△ **Each year, several million people go whale watching. From the deck of a leisure boat, tourists enjoy the animals in their natural environment.**

△ **Containers are loaded onto a ship in the port of Riga.**

Transportation

With the growth of the air industry, overseas travel by boat is much less common than it was even 50 years ago. However, about 90 percent of the world's heavy goods still travel overseas by boat rather than by air. Much of the fruit, vegetables, and meat we eat has reached our shores in large refrigerated metal containers. They are loaded onto cargo ships or are carried by trucks on ferries.

△ **The Panama Canal links the Atlantic and Pacific oceans. It is an invaluable shortcut for ships that have to travel between these oceans.**

Policing the world

Nuclear submarines patrol quietly below the sea surface and monitor the world's sea traffic. They also protect their own and other countries' national interests and guard against potential enemy attacks. The most powerful nations of the world maintain large navies. As the Gulf War of 1991 demonstrated, these navies can launch devastating attacks by air as well as by sea.

△ **Aircraft carriers, such as the USS *Kitty Hawk*, play a central role in today's larger navies. Their heavily armed warplanes can attack targets at long range.**

The future of the oceans

Renewable energy • Genetic engineering • Medicine

We must learn to manage our use of the oceans if we are to keep the seas healthy. The oceans already provide plenty of invaluable resources, and many future opportunities lie within them. Electrical energy can be generated, valuable metals can be harvested, and medical drugs are being developed from chemicals in sea creatures.

△ **Green-lipped mussels contain a chemical that helps relieve the symptoms of rheumatoid arthritis.**

Harnessing clean energy

The sea offers seemingly boundless opportunities for generating electrical energy. We have yet to find ways of harnessing the enormous power of ocean currents, but mills powered by tidal rises and falls have been working in Europe for hundreds of years. Differences in temperature between deep water and surface water could be used to turn gases into liquid and back again to power turbines that generate electricity. Such ocean thermal-energy conversion systems (OTECs) are being tested in Hawaii and elsewhere.

New drugs, new organisms

Thousands of coral reef animals are currently being tested for use in drugs that might combat cancer, AIDS, and a host of other medical conditions. At least two dozen useful drugs have been found in the last ten years, and many more wait to be discovered. Meanwhile, the genetic engineering of farmed fish and shellfish seems set to create animals that will grow more quickly, taste better, be less susceptible to disease, and will have a longer shelf life in the supermarket.

△ **The tide-driven turbines of the Rance Estuary Barrage in France can generate half a million kilowatts of electricity, enough to provide power for tens of thousands of homes.**

FAQs

FAQs

Why is the **sea salty**?

△ A scientist examining a seawater sample. The amount of salt in seawater, its salinity, is measured chemically or electrically.

Take a mouthful of seawater and it tastes salty. The salt in seawater is mostly common salt, or sodium chloride, but there are hundreds of other chemicals, too. In fact, most of the chemicals on Earth are found in one form or another in the sea. Many are dissolved out of rocks and soil on land and eventually find their way into the oceans through rivers. Volcanoes on land and volcanic vents underwater add chemicals as well. Some of the chemicals in seawater even arrive from space.

? Why is the sea blue?

Sunlight contains all the colors of the rainbow. When sunlight shines on clear seawater, water molecules scatter and reflect blue wavelengths of light, making the sea appear blue. Other wavelengths of light—reds, yellows, greens, and so on—are absorbed by seawater and so are not seen. Water molecules in the sky produce a similar effect, which is why the clear sky appears blue.

? Why does the sea change color?

The sea is not always blue. In fact, it can be almost any color. Changes in shade are caused by particles floating in the water. The particles may be living organisms, such as microscopic plankton, or they may be small particles of rock or soil swept into the sea. Pollution can cause the sea to change color, such as when sewage is pumped out to sea. Sometimes the reflection of the sky colors the water. A glorious sunset can turn the sea fiery red.

▽ Here, **in the vicinity of** St. Marc of Gonaives, Haiti, the previous night's heavy rain has swept topsoil into the rivers. The soil particles are staining the sea brown.

? What is a red tide?

A red tide happens when some kinds of microscopic plant plankton multiply in such numbers that their bodies turn the sea red. Sometimes, red tides contain chemicals that are poisonous. Strangely, most invertebrates (animals without backbones) are not harmed by these poisons. So shellfish can feed on the plant plankton and take in and store the chemicals unharmed. But fish—or people— that eat the shellfish may become ill or even die.

How do scientists study the ocean floor?

Amazingly, scientists have seen more of the Moon's surface, and in greater detail, than they have of the deep-ocean floor. Most of the ocean floor is several miles below the sea surface, and penetrating this depth of water is not easy. There are great dangers and expense in taking people to such depths. However, new technologies, from sonar to robot vehicles, are now crossing this barrier and revealing the seafloor as never before.

▽ A scuba diver with scooter and video conducts a scientific survey. This is usually done at depths of less than 150 feet.

? Why is sonar so useful in studying the ocean floor?

Underwater, sound travels much farther than light. So scientists who want to "see" large areas of ocean floor use sonar (**SO**und **N**avigation **A**nd **R**anging). Modern side-scan sonars, such as TOBI and GLORIA, are towed behind research vessels and record the shape of thousands of square miles of seafloor in a single day. By making controlled explosions and analyzing the returning sound (seismic surveying), scientific instruments can even examine the nature of the rock below the ocean floor. Drills are then used to take samples to analyze the rock for age and structure. The rock's sediment layers tell us about the past history of the ocean.

GLORIA

△ The GLORIA system of side-scanning sonar can survey an area of seafloor nearly the size of Connecticut in a single day.

△ Geologists use hollow drills to extract cores of rock from the seabed.

◁ A satellite image of the Earth shows the huge areas of water that cover the globe.

▷ **Radar altimetry** uses radio waves to map the sea surface and the shape of seafloor hidden below.

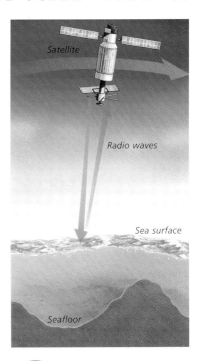

Satellite

Radio waves

Sea surface

Seafloor

How are satellites helpful in studying the ocean floor?

Some remote-sensing space satellites bounce radio waves off the sea surface. The time taken for radio waves to leave and return gives a precise measure of the satellite's height above the sea. This also gives a reading of sea level. The sea surface has dips and bumps that mirror the seafloor far below. Where there is a deep trench, the sea surface is slightly lower than normal, and where there is an undersea ridge or volcano, the sea is slightly raised. So taking measurements of sea level also tells scientists about the shape of the ocean floor below.

What is the difference between a submersible, an AUV, and an ROV?

A submersible is a small underwater craft than carries one or more people. An ROV, or remotely operated vehicle, is a robot vehicle operated from a distance by a submersible pilot or a ship's control room. In 1985–86, Robert Ballard and his team used the submersible *Alvin* and the ROVs *Argo* and *Jason* to explore the wreck of the *Titanic*. An AUV, or autonomous underwater vehicle, is a robot vehicle that operates alone without outside control. It trundles along the ocean floor for weeks or months on end gathering data.

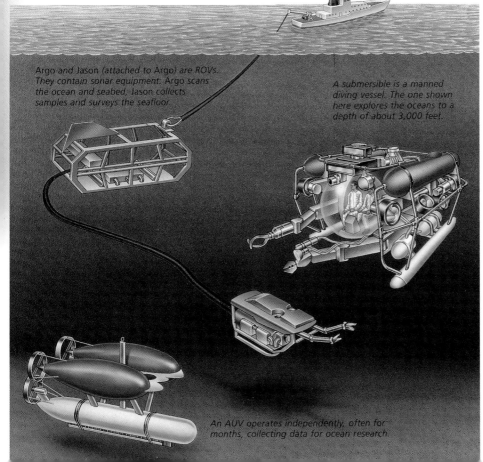

Argo and Jason (attached to Argo) are ROVs. They contain sonar equipment. Argo scans the ocean and seabed. Jason collects samples and surveys the seafloor.

A submersible is a manned diving vessel. The one shown here explores the oceans to a depth of about 3,000 feet.

An AUV operates independently, often for months, collecting data for ocean research.

How do ocean floor studies tell us about the extinction of the dinosaurs?

In 1980, scientists Luis and Walter Alvarez suggested that the dinosaurs became extinct because a giant meteorite struck the Earth about 65 million years ago. Sonar studies of the ocean floor have pinpointed the likely impact site. It is a sediment-covered undersea crater in the Gulf of Mexico. Here, seafloor samples of the right age show signs of meteorite impact.

Who
owns the sea?

Until the 17th century, those countries with large powerful navies took control of as much sea as they could. After this time, many nations agreed that everybody should be free to travel over the sea far from land, but that use of the sea close to shore should be controlled by the nearest country. In 1994 a Law of the Sea came into force. Coastal nations have control of a strip of "territorial sea" that extends up to 12 nautical miles from shore. Beyond this, they can fish, dredge, and drill in an "exclusive economic zone" up to 200 nautical miles from shore.

▷ **This diagram** shows the full range of national maritime (ocean) claims as agreed at the 1982 Law of the Sea Convention.

▽ **In historical times,** a country's 3-nautical-mile-wide territorial water could be protected by cannon fire from the land nearby.

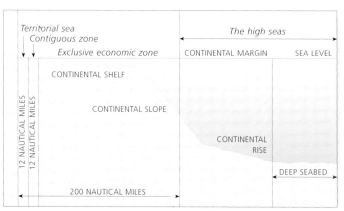

Territorial sea
Contiguous zone
Exclusive economic zone
The high seas
CONTINENTAL MARGIN   SEA LEVEL
CONTINENTAL SHELF
12 NAUTICAL MILES
12 NAUTICAL MILES
CONTINENTAL SLOPE
CONTINENTAL RISE
DEEP SEABED
200 NAUTICAL MILES

❓**W**hat does "freedom of the high seas" mean?

Since the 1600s, many nations have agreed that the high seas—the deep sea far beyond land—are open to anyone who can reach them and make use of them. This still holds, but the deep-ocean floor contains mineral riches that are the inheritance of all nations. Permission to mine must be obtained from the International Seabed Authority.

❓**W**hat is territorial water?

Until the early 1900s, many nations claimed a 3-nautical-mile strip of sea around their coastline—their territorial water—which they protected fiercely. Local people could fish these waters, but those of other nationalities needed permission. By the 1950s, some countries were claiming territorial waters more than 50 nautical miles wide, and this caused disputes between fishing nations. This was one reason why nations met to decide on an international law of the sea.

What are fishing disputes?

Fishing disputes are arguments between countries about who has the right to fish where, when, and by what means. Navies or fishery authorities sometimes capture fishing boats during such disputes. For example, in March 1995 the Spanish trawler *Estai* was seized by Canadian fisheries officers while fishing on the Grand Banks. Canada claimed that the *Estai* was catching turbot beyond the legally allowed catch limit. In 1998, five Egyptian fishing boats were captured after entering Yemeni waters without permission.

△ Illegal fishing continues to spark disputes over fishing rights.

▽ There have been many stories written about the adventures of pirates on the high seas. The real life of a pirate was often dangerous and violent.

Were all pirates men?

No, they weren't. In the early 1700s, Irish-born Anne Bonny and English-born Mary Read were pirates on board "Calico" Jack Rackham's pirate sloop, *The William*, in the Caribbean. Mary Read was a sailor on board a merchant ship until it was captured by Rackham, and she joined his crew. Anne Bonny was Rackham's partner. Both women were fierce fighters. When captured in 1720, they were both found to be pregnant and were freed. Jack Rackham, however, was hanged.

Did women become pirate captains?

At least two did. Around 1530, Grace O'Malley commanded a small fleet that plundered ships off Ireland. Queen Elizabeth I of England arranged for O'Malley's ships to be seized. The pirate agreed to attack only England's enemies, and her ships were released. In the early 1800s, a formidable Chinese woman, Ching Shih, commanded a fleet of 1,500 pirate ships in the South China Sea.

What is the difference between a pirate and a privateer?

A pirate is the general name for a sailor who attacks ships illegally. A privateer was a person (or ship) given government permission to plunder merchant ships of enemy countries. Among the most famous privateers were Englishman Francis Drake, Scotsman William Kidd, and Frenchman François le Clerc.

How do fishermen **find fish**?

The splashing of feeding dolphins, seals, and diving birds shows that there are fish near the surface. To find deeper swimming fish, fishermen use advanced technology. Sensitive sonars called fish finders pinpoint features—sudden rises and falls—on the seafloor where fish are likely to gather. They even display the fish schools themselves. The boat's global positioning system (GPS) tells the captain where he found the fish, and he can return at another time.

▽ A Chinese fisherman in local waters hauls in his nets to check his catch.

◁ The captain of a deep-sea trawler monitors a large school of fish (white area on screen) that he has picked up on his echo-sounder.

What are an upwelling and a downwelling?

An upwelling is a region of the sea where cold, nutrient-rich water from the deep wells up to the surface. This happens, for example, where frequent winds blow offshore. Upwellings often support large populations of plankton and the fish that feed on them. At downwellings, by contrast, winds blow onshore, and warm surface water is pushed down to the depths. The surface water is clear because it supports few plankton. In warm seas, coral reefs are often found at downwellings.

How do we know how many fish to catch?

Scientists study the fish caught by fishermen and those they catch themselves. By examining the growth rings found in scales and ear bones, they can work out the age of a fish. This tells them how quickly the fish are growing and how many fish of each age are in the catch. Scientists can then calculate how many fish can be caught without affecting the overall population. Unfortunately, the success of a fish population's breeding varies from year to year, so it is very difficult to predict how many fish can be caught.

An upwelling

Offshore winds

A downwelling

Onshore winds

Northeast Atlantic
11,663,100

Northeast Pacific
2,790,700

Northwest Atlantic
2,048,600

Northwest Pacific
24,565,100

Mediterranean and Black Sea
1,493,100

West Central Atlantic
1,825,000

East Central Atlantic
3,553,400

East Central Pacific
1,668,200

West Central Pacific
8,943,800

Southwest Atlantic
2,651,900

Southeast Atlantic
1,080,900

East Indian Ocean
3,875,500

West Indian Ocean
4,092,000

Southeast Pacific
14,414,300

Southwest Pacific
828,300

Antarctica
96,100

Catch in tons
= 1,000,000

Where are most fish caught?

△ The major marine fishing areas of the world and their catch in tons (based on FAO data).

Over half of the world's marine fish are caught in the cool waters of the North Pacific, the North Atlantic, and off the west coast of South America. In these areas, cold water rich in nutrients rises to the surface. In spring and summer, this water fuels the growth of plant plankton. The phytoplankton trap sunlight and use the nutrients to grow and multiply. The plankton create abundant food supplies for many animals, including fish. At the beginning of the 21st century, the top five marine fishing nations were China, Peru, Chile, Japan, and the United States.

▷ A satellite image shows the tongue of cold water that extends from the Peruvian coast in a normal year. During El Niño, the tongue of cold water disappears. Years in which the tongue fails to develop at all are called El Niño years.

What is El Niño?

El Niño is Spanish for "the male child" and refers to the Christ Child. El Niño happens traditionally around Christmas off the coast of Peru. It is a change in sea currents that marks the end of the peak fishing season. A slackening of the trade winds causes the local upwelling to subside, and phytoplankton stop growing as quickly. The plankton-feeding anchovies then go elsewhere. El Niño events can occur earlier, with the result that anchovy fishing is poor in that year. Fishing is particularly bad in an El Niño year.

Why are so many fish populations overfished?

Even when scientists get their predictions right, the people who decide how many fish should be caught may not listen to them. Even if they do, fishing rules must be enforced, and in many cases this does not happen. Left unchecked, fishermen catch as many fish as possible, so fish populations become overfished.

What makes the sea dangerous?

▽ **This painting, by Charles Parsons,** is of the clipper ship *Comet* of New York. She got caught in a violent hurricane off Bermuda on a voyage to San Francisco.

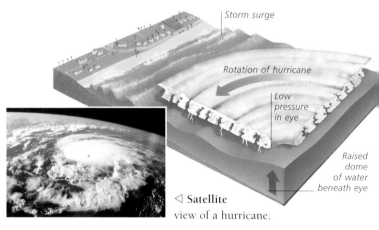

There are many dangers at sea—both above and below the waterline. The greatest danger is in taking the changing moods of the sea for granted and going out to sea unprepared. A flat calm sea can change into a cauldron of surging water and crashing waves within an hour. Seafarers must plan ahead and take account of likely weather conditions and many other factors that can affect their safety at sea. Most people who die at sea do so from cold or drowning after falling overboard, being shipwrecked, or being swept out to sea.

How are hurricanes born?

Hurricanes (also called typhoons) are powerful tropical storms born at sea. They form near the equator where warm moist air rises rapidly alongside descending cold air. This creates a swirling updraft which produces rain clouds. When the swirling winds reach 75 miles per hour, the storm is classified as a hurricane. At the center of a hurricane, seawater bulges, and at the edges, it surges. When hurricanes strike land, some cause tornadoes—narrow, destructive whirlwinds.

Storm surge

Rotation of hurricane

Low pressure in eye

Raised dome of water beneath eye

◁ **Satellite** view of a hurricane.

What causes giant waves?

Tsunami, Japanese for "harbor waves," can reach over 100 feet in height. Often mistakenly called tidal waves, they are caused by volcanoes and earthquakes that produce underwater shifts and avalanches. Tsunami travel at several hundred miles an hour and cause enormous devastation. An earthquake that occurred off the coast of south-central Chile in 1960 generated tsunami that claimed more than 400 lives.

◁ *The Breaking Wave off Kanagawa* by Hokusai shows a huge wave dwarfing Mount Fuji in the background.

Which marine creature is the most poisonous?

The most venomous creatures, in terms of the number of deaths they cause each year, are certain kinds of box jellyfish. They are found in some tropical coastal waters close to where rivers flow into the sea. There, they capture fish using their trailing stinging tentacles. Each year several dozen people die after accidentally colliding with them.

◁ **This box jellyfish may look harmless, but its sting is lethal.**

What is a rogue wave?

A rogue wave is a gigantic wave created on those rare occasions when two or more waves coincide. Rogue waves are probably the cause of some otherwise unexplained sinkings of sea vessels. In the ocean just off the southeast coast of Africa there is a "hot spot" for mysterious sinkings of oil tankers. Could rogue waves be the cause?

What is a waterspout?

A waterspout is really a tornado at sea. Its swirling column of air drags water from the sea surface and takes with it small animals and plants that live in the water. When the waterspout has run its course, its water—and the creatures in it—fall out of the sky. An unloading waterspout can flood and sink a boat. Waterspouts may account for some puzzling disappearances of vessels at sea.

▷ **This whirling column is a waterspout in the Java Sea.**

Which other poisonous marine creatures can kill?

The list of culprits includes sea snakes, fish armed with poisonous spines, and brightly patterned cone shells. One of the unlikeliest assassins is the blue-ringed octopus of Australia. Although this charming creature can fit in the palm of your hand, its bite can be lethal—the miniature octopus contains enough venom to kill ten people.

◁ **A tiny blue-ringed octopus sitting on a gloved hand.**

What makes sharks attack people?

In 1998, the International Shark Attack File (ISAF) recorded 58 shark attacks on people across the world. Six of these victims died. Great white sharks are among those responsible. They do not like the taste of human flesh, but they are curious and they mistake people for seals and other creatures they eat. Tiger sharks and bull sharks do, however, eat people. Attacks are most likely in warm, murky water where a person is splashing or behaving as though they are in distress. Blood in the water increases the chances of attack. But you are much more likely to be injured in an accident on the way to the beach than attacked by a shark once you get there.

Great white shark

Which
sea creatures can be
seen from space?

▽ **Australia's Great Barrier Reef** seen from space. It contains several hundred separate reefs.

The biggest marine creatures, and some of the smallest, are visible from space. When at the surface, bigger whales—of 50 feet or more—can be detected by remote-sensing satellites. At the other end of the scale, huge blooms of microscopic phytoplankton, stretching across many miles, can be seen because they stain large areas of the ocean. The Great Barrier Reef, made by countless billions of coral polyps, is possibly the biggest animal-made structure on Earth. Crew members of Apollo spacecraft could see this reef clearly from space.

?How are animals able to live at the bottom of the sea without being crushed?

The pressure in the very deep ocean is over one thousand times that at the surface. Unlike most other fish, deep-sea creatures don't have gas-filled swim bladders. In very deep water, gases are compressed by high pressure, and any air spaces would collapse. The tissues of deep-sea animals are mainly liquid or jellylike, and they hardly shrink when squeezed by pressure. Their skeletons are reduced because the surrounding high-pressure liquid provides so much support.

▷ **A humpback whale** can be detected from space when it comes to the sea's surface.

?Where do you find most marine life?

Most marine life is found near the top and at the bottom of the sea where food is abundant. In the sunlit zone, phytoplankton and seaweeds provide nourishment for a large community of animals. Eventually, almost all once-living material from surface waters will find its way to the seafloor, often passing through the stomachs of several creatures on the way. Offshore, upwellings are the most productive areas of surface water. In shallow water, sunlight reaches the seafloor, and luxuriant coral reefs or kelp forests may grow there.

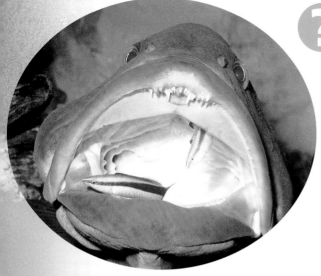

How do animals communicate underwater?

Sea creatures communicate by sight, sound, touch, taste, smell, and in other ways. Male humpback whales sing complicated songs to attract mates. Cuttlefish constantly change skin color to signal their state, turning black as a warning and flushing red to attract a mate. Female deep-sea angler fish leave a scent trail which males follow. Cleaner wrasse pick parasites and bits of damaged flesh from the surface of larger fish. The two communicate by touch, each reassuring the other, so the larger fish does not eat the smaller. Some fish, such as the stargazer, communicate with members of the same species using weak electrical signals.

△ A cleaner wrasse helps keep this coral cod parasite-free.

Why do whales sometimes strand themselves?

Whales occasionally strand themselves. One individual may have led the group astray, perhaps because it has a damaged navigation mechanism. Sometimes strandings occur where lines of magnetic force cross. Whales navigating along such lines may become confused. So strong are social ties that if one whale is injured and weak, the rest of the group may remain with it even if this endangers them.

How do creatures navigate in the open sea?

Sea creatures have an amazing range of senses. Many marine animals have a strong sense of smell, and they can "taste" the water and recognize where it comes from. They can distinguish underwater currents by their speed, depth, and direction, and by the plankton they contain. Many sea creatures can also sense magnetic fields produced by rocks below the sea. Salmon, for example, traveling from the sea to a river to breed, recognize ocean currents and use magnetic clues before homing in on the smell of their river. Adult turtles use an internal magnetic compass to steer themselves to their breeding grounds on remote beaches.

△ A rescue operation is underway to help these beached false killer whales.

▽ Newly hatched green turtles run to the sea attracted to the light reflected from the surface.

which

was the **biggest shipwreck**?

On the night of December 20, 1987, the Filipino ferry *Doña Paz* was crammed with people traveling to end-of-year celebrations. Registered to take about 1,500 passengers, the ferry was carrying more than double this number. At about 10 p.m., the oil tanker *Victor* collided with the *Doña Paz*. Kerosene spilled onto the water and immediately caught fire. In the fireball and explosions that followed over 3,000 people died—more than in any other peacetime shipwreck. Only 25 people survived.

▽ The Doña Paz functioned as a ferry before its collision with the tanker.

△ Sir Cloudesley's ships ran aground during a storm.

▷ The Titanic sank in 1912, with huge loss of life. The bow of the wreck is shown here.

Which sea disaster led to the invention of an accurate marine timepiece?

In 1707, four British ships commanded by Sir Cloudesley Shovell ran aground on the Isles of Scilly. They had miscalculated their longitude (east-west location). Measuring longitude accurately required keeping correct time. The tragedy encouraged the British government to offer a prize to the first person who could design an accurate timepiece for use at sea. In 1737, John Harrison built the first accurate ship's clock. Over the next 33 years, he gradually improved the design, but he had to wait until 1773 to receive the prize money.

◁ John Harrison's fourth marine chronometer, or timepiece, completed in 1759.

Why did people think that the ocean was five times deeper than it really was?

In the early 1800s, many British and American ships' captains took depth readings with a weight and line, which exaggerated the depth of the ocean. Ships drifted on currents, and when the weight and line were lowered, the ship moved from its original position. The rope curved through the water instead of hanging straight down. Also, the rope became waterlogged, making it difficult to tell when the weight had reached the seafloor. The rope piled up on the seabed and gave a false reading.

△ Many ships' captains of the early 1800s overestimated the ocean's depth.

Who said there was no life in the deep sea?

In the mid-1800s, Edward Forbes, a British naturalist, noted that the number of animals in seawater and on the ocean floor seemed to decrease with depth. Other scientists took this to mean that sea creatures ought to be absent entirely at great depths. In any case, they believed that creatures could not survive the great pressures and lack of light and oxygen in the deep sea. However, in 1860, an underwater telegraph cable was brought up from a depth of 6,000 feet. It was encrusted with marine life.

◁ This deep-sea cable is covered in marine life: soft corals, sponges, and sea lilies.

What
are the sea's greatest
mysteries?

Some of the sea's greatest mysteries are not mysteries at all, but fanciful inventions. The sea is so vast and so unpredictable that there are still many puzzles waiting to be solved. In the last 30 years alone, scientists have discovered two new species of whale and several kinds of shark. There are still plenty of secrets the ocean has yet to reveal, without our having to invent mysteries.

△ Sea monster? This manta ray is a large but harmless plankton-eating fish.

Are there sea monsters?

Stories of sea serpents and giant octopuses have captured people's imagination for centuries. The 60-foot giant squid was believed to be a myth until scientists examined intact specimens in the mid-1800s. Some sightings of huge snakelike creatures may be of the recently discovered 50-foot oarfish. Other giant sea creatures may yet be found.

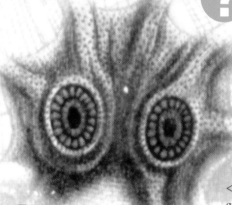

◁ A giant octopus attacks a galleon in this 19th-century print.

What happened on board the Mary Celeste?

In November 1872, the cargo vessel Mary Celeste was found drifting far out in the Atlantic with no one on board. The mystery was put down to piracy or sea monster attack. The most likely explanation is that the crew abandoned ship thinking it was about to sink or explode. Seawater was found in the hold, and its explosive cargo was raw alcohol.

What is the Bermuda Triangle?

The Bermuda Triangle is an area of sea believed, by some, to be linked with many unexplained disappearances. The most famous of these was the loss of Flight 19—five US Navy bombers—in 1945. Various writers claim that mysterious dangers in the Bermuda Triangle include giant whirlpools, methane gas explosions, magnetic disturbances, and abductions by extraterrestrials. However, when the facts are examined, the so-called Bermuda Triangle is the site of no more disappearances than would be expected for any ocean region with heavy air and sea traffic, turbulent and changeable weather, and treacherous currents and swells.

Bermuda

The Bermuda Triangle

Florida

Puerto Rico

JOBFILE

Jobfile

JOB TITLE:

Fisherman

JOB DESCRIPTION:

Jack is an experienced deck mate in a crew of eight aboard a 65-foot demersal trawler. Jack's fishing boat *North Star* operates out of Grimsby on the northeastern coast of England. This fishing port, like many others, has seen declining fortunes in the last 25 years.

NAME AND AGE:

*Jack Hargreaves, 44

*"Jack Hargreaves" is a fictional character.

What sort of fishing do you do?

I work on a pair trawler. It's one of two fishing boats that work together to haul a large trawl net—that's a net like a giant bag, which we drag along or close to the seabed. We catch demersal fish such as cod, haddock, plaice, and lemon sole.

Where do you fish?

Within a range of a few hundred miles, we go to the areas where the fish are and where the weather allows us to. That's mainly in the North Sea, and beyond that in the North Atlantic Ocean north of Scotland.

How long are you out at sea?

That really depends on the fishing and the weather. It's anything between a few days and two weeks. Sometimes it can take us three days to reach the fishing grounds and three days to return, and that's before we do any fishing. In the old days (20 years ago), if we had a great catch, we'd come back to port after just a few days with our holds full. Nowadays, we're likely to be out for ten days and come back with only a moderate catch. If the weather's bad, that can either make us stay out longer, until it clears, or it might make us return earlier.

FISHING WATERS

Trawlers about 65–80 feet in length, such as this one from Norway, may have to travel several hundred miles over a few days to reach the good fishing grounds.

HAULING IN THE NETS

In the past, fishing nets were towed and hauled by hand. Today, powerful winches and hydraulic machines haul and lift the huge trawl net, which may be many feet long. In pair trawling, one boat takes the net on board, but the two boats work together to tow and haul the net.

What does your job actually involve?

The fishing itself is, of course, just part of the job. We take turns to man the watch—steering the boat from the wheelhouse while other crew members catch up on their sleep. These days navigation is mainly electronic. There's not much I need to do other than hold to a course set by the chart plotter, keep an eye on the radar, and listen on the radio for storm warnings. I keep in touch by VHF with the other trawler of the pair.

How do you keep the fish fresh after they're caught?

We keep them chilled at 32°–40°F. They keep fresh for a week or more before they're sold when we get back to port.

What do you do with the fish you can't use?

The trash fish (ones we can't use) go back overboard. Some fish and shellfish, such as crabs, lobsters, and shrimp, we catch in such small numbers that we can't really sell them. We cook them on board and

our work. Echo-sounders and fish finders mean we can see the features on the seafloor, where fish gather, and higher up in the water we can even see the schools of fish themselves. But it's the overfishing that has been the biggest problem for fishermen all over the world. We have to travel much farther afield to find fish, and there are fewer to catch. Twenty-five years ago, there were 29 sets of pair trawlers working just from Grimsby. Now there is only one set left.

SPRAYING THE FISH

After the fish have been gutted, spraying them with seawater cleans them. In hot weather this helps keep the fish cool and fresh.

PROCESSING BELOW DECK

On large factory ships, such as this 250-foot trawler, fish are processed into a variety of products. Larger fish are gutted, cleaned, and filleted. Smaller fish and offal are turned into fishmeal. The fish products are frozen and packaged on board, and the ship may remain at sea for many weeks.

At other times, I help keep the boat clean and in good working order. And, of course, there's shooting the net, handling the net once it comes in, and sorting the catch and processing it. We separate the fish by type and sift the good from the bad. We gut the fish, which makes them keep much longer. When we're catching reasonable amounts of fish, we can't afford to stop. If we do, the fish will most likely have moved on. At those times we work continuously, perhaps grabbing just two hours' sleep at a time.

eat them, or take them home. Because of the size of the mesh we use, we don't usually catch undersize fish, but sometimes, when sea conditions are bad and the pull on the net seesaws between tight and slack, the mesh opens and closes, and we do catch undersize fish.

How has fishing changed since you started 20 years ago?

Enormously. Of course, there is all the new technology that helps us to be more efficient in

PRESERVING FISH

These cod are being packed in ice to keep them chilled and fresh until they reach port. Fish are usually sold at a fish market within 24 hours of landing. They have various destinations: local stores and restaurants, or supermarkets hundreds of miles away.

What's the most unusual thing you've caught?

Once we caught three explosive mines! And they were modern ones, too—not from World War II. We reckon they'd fallen overboard from some warship. We had to cut the net. Another time we caught a dead minke whale. We had to cut that net, too. We'd probably have damaged our fishing gear, and the boat, trying to haul it in.

What's the worst thing to happen to you at sea?

I've been caught plenty of times at sea in force 8 and 9 gales. It's been touch and go, with the wind whipping around us and waves crashing right over the boat. I've lost friends who've been swept overboard. One boat in our fleet did capsize and all the crew were lost. Even if you know exactly what you're doing, the sea is full of surprises.

Would you want your children to become fishermen?

No, I wouldn't. Both my children have got shore jobs. Young men have romantic ideas about fishing. Yes, it is a very tough and dangerous job. To be good at it takes a lot of stamina. You have to be strong to put up with the rough and often terrible conditions. Every time they go to sea, fishermen have to trust each other with their lives. It is not an easy way to make a living.

TENDING TO TRAWL NETS ON DECK

It is important that the nets on any fishing vessel are kept in good condition. Damaged nets affect the catch. Large trawl nets take a lot of maintenance and have to be stored carefully.

DANGERS ON THE DECK

When the net is being hauled in, the fishing line is under great strain, and any breakages of rope or machinery can result in parts flying through the air at high speed. There is always the danger of being swept overboard, particularly in rough seas, when the deck is slippery and the net is swaying.

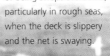

JOB TITLE:

Submariner

JOB DESCRIPTION:

John spends several months of the year underwater. He is a Naval officer and is specialized in ballistic missile submarines. He is currently responsible for making sure that the air inside one of the Navy's most advanced submarines is fit to breathe.

NAME AND AGE:

*John Farnsworth, 36

*"John Farnsworth" is a fictional character.

What kind of submarine do you work in?

I work in a strategic ballistic missile submarine—SSBN for short. It's powered by a nuclear reactor, which means we're not short of fuel. We can stay underwater for months at a time. Our most powerful weapons by far are the Trident nuclear missiles, which we can launch from underwater. Thankfully, we've never had to do that for real.

What does the submarine do?

Our two main jobs are surveillance and deterrence. For us, surveillance means keeping an eye on what's going on above and below the water. Deterrence means putting an enemy off attacking our nation or one of our allies. Just one of our Trident nuclear missiles has the power equivalent to dozens of the atomic bomb that was dropped on Hiroshima. We spend most of our time quietly patrolling the oceans. Very few people know where we are, or who or what we are watching.

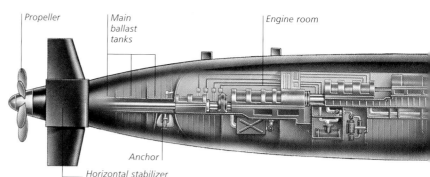

Propeller | Main ballast tanks | Engine room

Anchor

Horizontal stabilizer

What is a typical day like?

When we are on patrol, the submarine is operational 24 hours a day, so we work in shifts. It's easy to lose track of the real day and night when you are below the sea for a long time. To counteract the effect of this, we work in white light during the day and in red light during our artificial night. It is amazing how soon you adapt to this strange way of life. When we're on patrol, it's slightly eerie. We run quietly to avoid detection. No one raises his voice, slams a hatch, or carelessly drops anything.

How do you cope with being underwater for so long?

You get used to it. You wouldn't do this job if you suffered badly from claustrophobia (the fear of enclosed spaces). The worst part is being away from your family for months on end. You're only allowed a very short message from home about once a week. We combat boredom by working very hard and doing plenty of practice

MODERN SUBMARINE AT THE SURFACE

The USS *La Jolla*, a US nuclear-powered attack submarine, can travel at 30 knots at depths of up to 1,500 feet. The sub is armed with torpedoes, non-nuclear missiles, and mines.

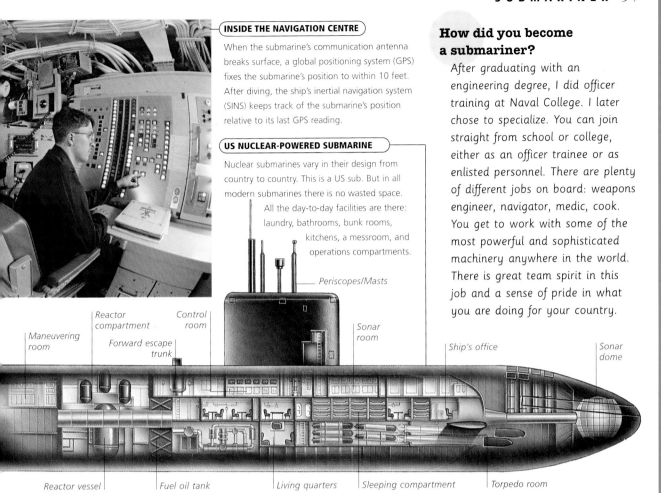

(INSIDE THE NAVIGATION CENTRE)

When the submarine's communication antenna breaks surface, a global positioning system (GPS) fixes the submarine's position to within 10 feet. After diving, the ship's inertial navigation system (SINS) keeps track of the submarine's position relative to its last GPS reading.

(US NUCLEAR-POWERED SUBMARINE)

Nuclear submarines vary in their design from country to country. This is a US sub. But in all modern submarines there is no wasted space. All the day-to-day facilities are there: laundry, bathrooms, bunk rooms, kitchens, a messroom, and operations compartments.

Periscopes/Masts

Maneuvering room

Reactor compartment

Forward escape trunk

Control room

Sonar room

Ship's office

Sonar dome

Reactor vessel

Fuel oil tank

Living quarters

Sleeping compartment

Torpedo room

How did you become a submariner?

After graduating with an engineering degree, I did officer training at Naval College. I later chose to specialize. You can join straight from school or college, either as an officer trainee or as enlisted personnel. There are plenty of different jobs on board: weapons engineer, navigator, medic, cook. You get to work with some of the most powerful and sophisticated machinery anywhere in the world. There is great team spirit in this job and a sense of pride in what you are doing for your country.

drills. When we leave the sub at the end of a mission, we're so used to seeing things close up, we can no longer focus at a distance. The effect soon wears off.

What do you do on board the submarine?

I'm the atmospheric control officer, which means I'm responsible for making sure the sub's air is fit to breathe. At six-hourly intervals the air is sampled and analyzed using special equipment. If an unwanted gas is present, we have to take corrective action very quickly.

Where do you get fresh food and fresh air from?

We keep our fresh food cool, but it runs out after several weeks. We carry massive supplies (enough for

135 men) of frozen and canned food. As for air, we filter and recycle it. We "scrub" the air through a chemical unit, which removes carbon dioxide, and oxygen is automatically added. We produce the oxygen by passing electricity through seawater.

What happens if there is an accident?

A submarine is a set of sealable compartments, each with its own atmosphere. In emergencies, you move to an escape compartment. If you have to abandon ship, you put on a special escape suit, which keeps you warm and allows you to breathe on the way up.

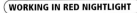

(WORKING IN RED NIGHTLIGHT)

The submarine crew work in artificial red nightlight when it is nighttime on the surface.

JOB TITLE:

Marine biologist

JOB DESCRIPTION:

Karen is a rare breed of marine biologist. She has lived and worked under the sea in Aquarius-2000, a fully operational underwater laboratory dedicated to research. We caught up with Karen as she was returning from a 10-day mission.

NAME AND AGE:

*Karen Driver, 34

*"Karen Driver" is a fictional character.

SEA URCHINS

These spiny creatures are a vital part of a coral reef community. They eat the algae that could smother the coral if left to grow.

Where do you work?

I work at a university, where I divide my time between teaching marine biology, diving to carry out my research, experimenting in the lab, and analyzing data and writing scientific papers. For the past ten days I've been an aquanaut in Aquarius. The underwater lab is anchored in 55 feet of water about 4 miles off the Florida Keys. I've been doing two three-hour dives a day among the coral nearby.

SIDE VIEW OF AQUARIUS

Aquarius looks like a blunt-ended yellow submarine anchored on a large metal plate. Inside, it feels like a high-tech motor home. The working and living space is very small.

CORAL FEEDING EXPERIMENT

A scientist checks and adjusts the equipment used in a coral feeding experiment. Scientists learn a lot about the marine environment from the research that they carry out from Aquarius.

What about your research?

My interest is in marine ecology—studying how marine organisms get along together. My specialty is studying sea urchins and their effect on the populations of algae they feed on. Sea urchins are greedy eaters. Without them, algae can overgrow and smother and kill a coral reef. We're trying to find out how quickly the algae grow. We're running experiments to grow them in differing amounts of shade. We're also seeing how much algae the sea urchins eat and whether algae regrows elsewhere when it is scattered by fish as they bite chunks off and spit them out.

What are the advantages of working from an undersea laboratory?

The biggest advantage is the extra time we can spend on the seafloor carrying out experiments and making observations. If we scuba dive from the surface, we can only spend an hour or so at 65–100-foot depths before we have to return to the surface. Because of the pressure change, we have to rise slowly. This allows the pressurized gas to bubble out of the bloodstream. The process is called decompression. Aquarius is at the same pressure as its surroundings, so we don't have to decompress at the end of a dive. This means we can make two three-hour dives in a day. We only have to decompress at the end of the 10-day mission. Living in Aquarius, we can monitor the reef day and night—it gives us a much better understanding of the underwater world.

What is Aquarius like inside?

It has three compartments, or locks. We get in and out through the wet porch. Here we put on and take off our diving gear and can have a hot shower. The next compartment is the science area, where we have our onboard computers and do most of our recording and analysis of results. The final compartment is the living quarters. At the end of this are six closely packed bunk beds where we sleep. It's lovely lying in bed looking out through the viewport at the fish swimming by outside. We have a small kitchen—most of our food is freeze-dried or microwaved.

Are the public allowed inside?

No, they're not. Not only do we all have hundreds of hours of diving experience, but we also plan the mission months in advance. We then do five days of intensive training just

INSIDE AQUARIUS

This view is of the main compartment of Aquarius looking toward the entry lock (where the wet porch is). Here, the scientists do most of their analysis and recording of data. They can also get a good view of the sea from the viewports.

before the mission. The four scientists and two technicians on board each have specific jobs to do. Aquarius is very much a working space. With its backup team on shore, Aquarius costs about $10,000 a day to run.

What changes are happening to the reef? Is pollution a problem?

Coral bleaching—when hard corals eject their algal partners and die—is becoming more common. High water temperatures and raised levels of ultraviolet light are at least partly responsible, and global warming and the thinning ozone layer may be involved. Sewage and other forms of pollution and interference are on the increase. Studying the changes is important. That's why we're here.

CORAL REEF PLANTS

At night, many of the daytime reef animals hide away and another group emerges. During the day, some corals look like lumps of stone, but at night thousands of brightly colored feeding tentacles cover what hours earlier seemed like lifeless rock.

SEE ALSO

JOB TITLE:

Marine archaeologist

JOB DESCRIPTION:

Marjorie is part of a skilled team that finds, records, and excavates historical sites at sea, ranging from shipwrecks to submerged settlements. The job involves interpreting the finds and publishing scientific reports based on them. The work sometimes includes preserving historical objects for public display.

NAME AND AGE:

*Marjorie Cleaver, 44

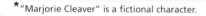

*"Marjorie Cleaver" is a fictional character.

What does your work on a site involve?

Marine archaeology, like archaeology on land, is very much a team effort. Usually, six or more people—sometimes dozens—are involved in excavating a site. Recently, most of my work has been with Tudor (16th-century) finds in shallow waters off the British coast. I've worked with teams that have found ships' hulls, cannons, longbows, silver and pewter plates, flatware, dishes, leather clothing, and, yes, plenty of gold and silver objects. But what is most important is the arrangement of these items on the site. How did they come to be where they are? If it was a shipwreck, can we recreate how the people lived before disaster struck? It is fascinating how much you can learn from these finds.

RETRIEVING ARTIFACTS

Historical objects are called artifacts. Before they are recovered from a shallow-water site, the area is marked off with a grid of tape or aluminum. The exact position of each artifact within the grid is recorded—by notetaking, drawing, or video or still photography. Only then is the artifact removed.

CLEARING SAND FROM A SHIPWRECK

A giant vacuum-cleanerlike device called an air dredge is being used to suck up sand from a shipwreck site. The sucked-up water and sediment is usually filtered through mesh to recover fragments and small objects of interest.

CAREFULLY BAGGING ARTIFACTS

The exact position of each artifact is recorded before it is removed. Each object is tagged and numbered. The details are entered into a computer database, which generates a three-dimensional map of the site, displaying the recovered artifacts in their original positions.

Are you a treasure hunter?

No. Not in the sense that I find treasures that I can make lots of money from. Treasures, for me, are things that tell us more about the past, about how people lived centuries ago. A knife and fork, a belt buckle, or a longbow and arrow are worth as much as, or more than, gold coins in terms of the archeological information they give us. It is the jigsaw puzzle of objects we find at a site that is valuable, not just the individual objects themselves.

What are the difficulties doing archaeology underwater rather than on land?

The problems you encounter are very different. Marine archaeology is more difficult and more hazardous because you are having to work under water. In shallow water, we usually scuba dive to investigate the site. Off the British coast, water temperatures are often 50°F or less and visibility may be less than 3 feet. And there are also winds, waves, and currents to contend with. Excavating a site is often difficult, time-consuming, and

expensive. You need to record everything you find—what it is and exactly where you found it. That is quite easy on land, but more difficult in water. Then, if you recover objects and take them out of their watery environment, your problems are only just beginning. In air, the underwater finds usually rapidly disintegrate or corrode unless you take special measures. On the plus side, the marine environment can preserve some objects really well, and the site is less accessible to looters. An undisturbed site can be like a "time capsule" telling you an awful lot about life in another era.

How do you know where to look?

We use historical material and modern technology. Historical records—old charts and company records, for example—provide clues about where to look for shipwrecks. Artifacts may be washed up on shore or revealed at low tide. Since the late 1960s, side-scan sonars have been used. They reveal unexpected bumps and dips on the seabed that betray the presence of a shipwreck. Side-scan sonar was used to discover the site of HMS Mary Rose in 1967. In 1985, the RMS Titanic, lying in about 2½ miles of water, was discovered using an underwater remotely operated vehicle (ROV) called Argo armed with video cameras. Towed or hand-held magnetometers detect local variations in magnetic fields and reveal buried metal. Modern sub-bottom sonars can detect objects buried on the seabed, metal or not. Sometimes it's just a matter of chance—a diver seeing a wooden beam or a cannon lying on the seafloor.

Are you a diver?

Yes. Most marine archaeologists are. I've completed over 600 dives since I was 18, and I have both sports and professional diving qualifications. Scuba diving is only practical down to a maximum depth of about 165 feet. Beyond that, you need more advanced training and a special deep-diving suit. Beyond 2,000 feet, you would need to use a submersible or a robot vehicle.

How do you get things up from the bottom of the sea?

You have to uncover them first. Fine layers of sediment can be removed with a brush, a small fan, or a jet-wash. Loose sediment can be sucked up using an air dredge (an underwater vacuum cleaner). Small to medium-sized objects are raised in a net or crate slung below an air-filled bag called an air-lift. Heavier objects such as part of a ship's hull are winched to the surface by rope, cradled in a sling or in a custom-made frame. It costs a lot to raise large objects from the deep and preserve them, so we often map a site and remove some of its artifacts, but leave the wreck and its fittings in their resting place on the seabed.

How do you preserve things once you've found them?

Objects must be cleaned first. Anything lying on the seabed is usually caked with the chalky encrustations of barnacles, coral, shellfish, or worms, which may need to be removed chemically. Metal items can be treated by electrolysis to slowly dislodge encrustations. As for preserving artifacts, methods include freeze-drying and chemical treatment, depending on what the object is.

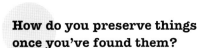

RAISING OBJECTS IN A CRATE

These ceramic vessels are being retrieved from a ship wrecked in 1025 in the Aegean Sea off the coast of Turkey.

WINCHING UP RECOVERED ARTIFACTS

This bronze muzzle-loading gun is from the wreck of the *Mary Rose*, King Henry VIII's flagship, which sank near Plymouth in 1545. Since the wreck's discovery in 1967, over 20,000 artifacts have been recovered, including longbows, arrows, and a surgeon's chest containing medical instruments and potions.

How do you become a marine archaeologist?

First of all, you need to have a degree in Archaeology. Then you need to specialize in Marine Archaeology, usually by taking an advanced degree—a masters or a doctorate. Almost all marine archaeologists now need to have a professional diving qualification, too. This allows you greater choice in what you can do within the scope of your work. So you are looking at four to seven years of specialized academic training to get the qualifications you will need to take up marine archaeology as a career.

One final question, does Atlantis really exist?

By that I suppose you mean an ancient but advanced culture that sank beneath the waves some 11,000 years ago? I don't believe there is any reliable evidence for its existence. None of the proposed sites—those in the Atlantic Ocean or others such as Santorini or Antarctica—pass close inspection. It was Plato, the ancient Greek philosopher, who first wrote about this culture. I think he made it up, or was misinformed, and romantics have jumped on the bandwagon ever since. It certainly is a fascinating idea, and I'm willing to be proved wrong.

PRESERVATION: FREEZE-DRYING

Leather artifacts and small wooden items, such as these from the *Mary Rose*, can be freeze-dried. This instantaneously turns their water content into gas. This prevents them from rotting, shrinking, and distorting, which would happen if they were dried slowly. Sometimes they are chemically treated before freeze-drying so some of the water has already been replaced.

PRESERVING THE RECOVERED SHIP

Large wooden items, such as this half-hull of the *Mary Rose*, are sprayed with cold freshwater to keep them moist and to prevent bacteria and fungi from growing on them. In the case of the *Mary Rose*, after ten years the sprinkle of water was replaced by a spray of the waxy preservative polyethylene glycol. In another 20 years, this substance will have replaced the water in the wood and spraying can stop.

FINAL DISPLAYED OBJECTS

Once the artifacts have been treated, they need to be kept under special conditions—at the correct temperature and humidity, and in the right gas environment. The display case needs to keep out organisms—insects, fungi, and bacteria—that could cause decay. The artifacts also need to have labels plus a commentary that explains what they are.

Leather shoe

Ceramic jars

SEE ALSO

JOB TITLE:

Beach lifeguard

JOB DESCRIPTION:

A lifeguard is legally responsible for safeguarding swimmers and other beach-users. The job doesn't involve just rescuing people—far from it. It mainly involves making sure that people don't get into trouble in the first place. That includes giving advice and making people aware of the do's and don'ts of beach safety.

NAME AND AGE:

*Sam Spooner, 21

*"Sam Spooner" is a fictional character.

Surfers only
No swimmers

Beach patrolled
by lifeguards

KEEPING A WATCH FOR DANGER

There is much more to being a lifeguard than you think. You have to be good at working in a team, but you also need to work on your own initiative. If there is an emergency, you've got to make quick judgments. You always radio for backup, but you may have to take command of the situation yourself. That means winning the confidence of those around you.

What training do you need to be a lifeguard?

The basic training is a blend of theory and practice done over several weeks or months. Of course, you need to be a strong swimmer. In pool training you learn how to rescue people under many different circumstances. You master first aid and how to revive people. You discover how to identify the different factors to take into account on a particular beach: the currents, tides, weather, the shape of the beach, and so on. You learn to use equipment: the torpedo buoy, rescue skis, a Malibu board. In open-water training you have to show that you can put all the pieces of your training together, that you can rescue people without endangering yourself or others. If you stay in lifeguarding, you never stop training and learning. You go on refresher courses, and you're always learning new skills.

SAFETY FLAGS AND SYMBOLS

Lifeguards work with other emergency and information services to make sure warnings and advice are provided for beach users. On popular public beaches, a flag system shows where and when it is safe to swim.

Is the job as glamorous as it seems to be on TV?

Is it like Baywatch, you mean? Well, in most places it isn't except, perhaps, in high summer when it's really sweltering and the surf is up. You've got a responsible job to do. People are depending on you. You've got to win people's respect. You've got to stay focused. You can't just wander about enjoying yourself, talking to your pals. I suppose being a lifeguard does give you an added attractiveness. It isn't easy, but it is a great job.

Surely it's a summer job? What do you do for the rest of the year?

Some lifeguards are volunteers, while others, like me, are paid. I lifeguard in summer. The rest of the year I'm a university student. Older lifeguards tend to have other jobs and lifeguard only at weekends or to cover special events.

FACTFILE

Factfile

Ocean facts

Seawater

There is no shortage of seawater. For each person on our planet, there are more than 60 billion gallons of seawater. If the Earth's surface were leveled so all raised areas were flattened and hollows were filled, the Earth would be covered in seawater to a depth of 1¾ miles.

Salinity

The saltiness of seawater, its salinity, hardly varies from one ocean to another. It is usually about 35 parts of salt in 1,000 parts of seawater. When seawater is diluted by freshwater from rivers or melting ice, the salinity falls. When seawater becomes concentrated by evaporation—such as in rockpools or tropical lagoons—salinity rises.

△ Bora Bora is a South Pacific island surrounded by a barrier reef. In the island's coral lagoon, water evaporates and the seawater left behind becomes saltier (more saline).

Pacific Ocean

Area:	63,800,000 square miles
Widest point:	11,000 miles
Average depth:	14,000 feet
Deepest point:	36,200 feet (in the Mariana Trench)
Main features:	• The Mariana Trench is the world's deepest trench • San Andreas Fault (270 miles long) • East Pacific Ridge (spreading ridge), 6,500–10,000 feet high and 2,175 miles long

Atlantic Ocean

Area:	31,835,000 square miles
Widest point:	6,000 miles
Average depth:	11,000 feet
Deepest point:	27,500 feet (in the Puerto Rico Trench)
Main features:	• The Puerto Rico Trench is the world's second deepest trench • Mid-Atlantic Ridge is 7,000 miles long and up to 13,000 feet high. It runs the length of the Atlantic, north to south.

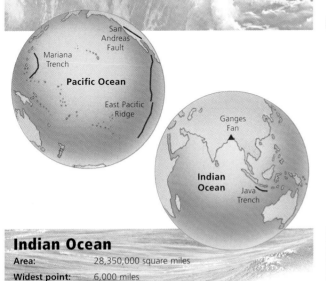

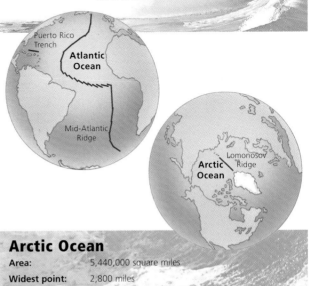

Indian Ocean

Area:	28,350,000 square miles
Widest point:	6,000 miles
Average depth:	12,760 feet
Deepest point:	24,450 feet (in the Java Trench)
Main features:	• Ganges Fan is the world's largest sediment fan at 930 miles across

Arctic Ocean

Area:	5,440,000 square miles
Widest point:	2,800 miles
Average depth:	3,240 feet
Deepest point:	18,050 feet (on the Polar Abyssal Plain)
Main features:	• Lomonosov Ridge, the site of seafloor spreading • This ocean is unusual in having the widest continental shelf (north of Eurasia), 1,000 miles across

Ocean facts

Polar oceans—the Arctic

- The Arctic Ocean is almost entirely surrounded by land.

- Even in summer, more than half of its area is covered in ice. Pack ice forms when seawater freezes.

- Arctic icebergs are created (calved) when they break off glaciers. Around 10,000 icebergs are calved in and around the Arctic Ocean each year, and more than 300 drift into shipping lanes and cause a hazard. Typically, the tip of an iceberg—the part we can see—is only 10–20 percent of the whole. The remaining 80–90 percent lies below the surface.

▽ An icebreaker plows through pack ice.

△ The polar bear is the largest predator living on the Arctic ice floes.

Antarctica

- Antarctica, at the South Pole, is a continent surrounded by an ocean.

- It is the most untouched part of our planet. It is bitingly cold. Coastal temperatures average -22°F and only rise above freezing point in the Antarctic summer.

- The waters of the Southern Ocean around Antarctica, despite the cold, teem with life. Krill feed on the phytoplankton and in turn are eaten by fish, squid, whales, penguins, and seals.

- Antarctic icebergs break off the Antarctic ice sheet and are flat-topped. In March 1996, one was created that was 48 miles long and 23 miles wide.

▽ Scientists from the British Antarctica Survey in their camp.

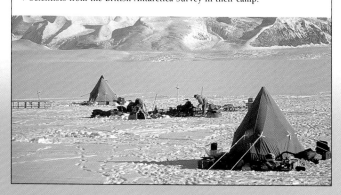

△ This Weddell seal in Antarctica has made a breathing hole in the ice. It gnaws at the hole to prevent it from freezing over.

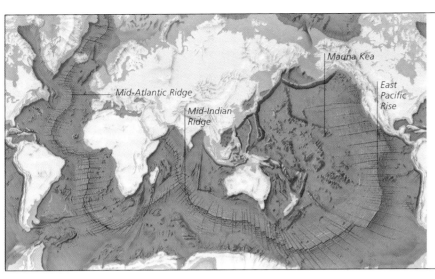

Mountains in the ocean

- The world's longest mountain chain starts in the Arctic Ocean, meanders down the center of the Atlantic Ocean, skirts Africa in the Indian Ocean, and then runs below Australia before crossing the Pacific Ocean. It is the Mid-Ocean Ridge system and is more than three times longer than the Himalayas, Andes, and Rockies combined.

- Mauna Kea, an inactive volcano on Hawaii, is really the tallest mountain on Earth. Although its peak is only 13,796 feet above sea level (Mount Everest is 29,026 feet above sea level), Mauna Kea rises from the ocean floor and from base to peak is 33,465 feet tall.

◁ The Mid-Ocean Ridge system is more than 24,850 miles long and extends from the Arctic Ocean to the eastern Pacific.

Giant aquariums

Containing part of the ocean and its creatures in a large tank is no easy matter. Yet public aquariums are becoming increasingly popular, and each year several new ones are built. One tank in California's Monterey Bay Aquarium is 34¾ feet deep and contains one million gallons of seawater. Its acrylic viewing window is 12½ inches thick.

The Pacific "Ring of Fire" display in Japan's Osaka Aquarium contains 14 separate exhibits that depict living communities in and around the Pacific Ocean. It harbors more than 35,000 specimens drawn from 380 species.

▷ Visitors at the Monterey Bay Aquarium can see sharks, turtles, and barracuda in this gigantic tank.

Ocean creatures

In 1977, American scientists traveling along a Pacific ridge in the submersible *Alvin* stumbled across an amazing sight. Packing the slopes around hot water (hydrothermal) vents were giant tubeworms, about 3 feet long, and huge mussels and clams 10 inches long. The remarkable community of animals was sustained by chemicals spewing out of the vents. Since then, dozens of such hydrothermal vent communities have been discovered. So far, scientists know of fewer than 200,000 deep-sea creatures (many of microscopic size), but several million different kinds are believed to live in or on the bottom of the sea.

◁ Male emperor penguins look after the newly hatched chicks. They, and their young, survive winter blizzards at -75°F.

SEE ALSO
Blue planet	10–11
Restless land and sea	12–13
Glossary	78–81

The changing oceans

Overfishing

For hundreds of years, fishermen have been overfishing one fish population after another. The Food and Agriculture Organization of the United Nations (FAO) recently estimated that of seventeen major world fisheries, thirteen were either being fished to their limit or were overfished. When a fish population collapses and few, if any, fish are caught, the fishermen are put out of business or must seek fish elsewhere. There is no guarantee that the fish population will recover. To take one recent example (illustrated in the bar chart below), overfishing in the Northwest Atlantic resulted in the collapse of cod and haddock fisheries in the early 1990s. When major Canadian and American fishing grounds were closed, 40,000 fishermen and other workers lost their jobs.

△ Cannery Row, Monterey Bay: in the 1930s, thirty businesses processed fish here. In the 1950s, many closed down when the California sardine fishery collapsed.

The estimated population numbers of types of whale before and after intensive whaling		
	1900	**1999**
Blue whale	275,000	Less than 5,000
Bowhead whale	More than 50,000	Less than 8,500
Humpback whale	150,000	20,000
Fin whale	More than 500,000	120,000
Northern right whale	10,000* (*Original population in 17th century. Most of the depletion took place before 1900.)	350

▽ Inuit subsistence whalers butcher a bowhead whale. Some traditional communities are allowed to kill a few whales each year.

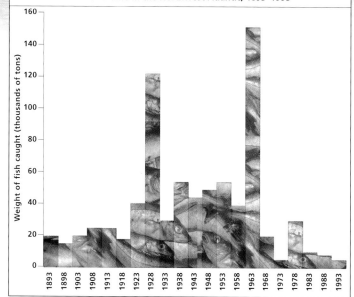

Catches of haddock from George's Bank and the Gulf of Maine in the Northwest Atlantic, 1893–1993

Weight of fish caught (thousands of tons) — 0, 20, 40, 60, 80, 100, 120, 140, 160

1893, 1898, 1903, 1908, 1913, 1918, 1923, 1928, 1933, 1938, 1943, 1948, 1953, 1958, 1963, 1968, 1973, 1978, 1983, 1988, 1993

Overhunting

Catching whales has always been a brutal business. Whalers harpoon an animal that struggles for life and is eventually overcome by exhaustion and loss of blood.

By the early 1900s, whaling had become so efficient that some whale populations nearly became extinct. Whalers had to find new hunting grounds. European and North American sailors traveled to the Southern Ocean to hunt the whales there. Slow-moving humpback whales were hunted first, then the largest whales—blue and fin. When these populations were exhausted, smaller whales—sei and minke—were hunted. It was not until 1986 that a worldwide moratorium (temporary halt) on whale hunting was introduced. Many whale populations were at dangerously low levels. Norway and Japan still catch several hundred whales a year despite objections by other countries. However, populations of several whales (e.g. humpbacks) are making a gradual recovery.

Extinction

In the sea, as well as on land, animals and plants are dying out at an increasing rate because of human interference. We pollute the sea, alter or remove marine habitats, and hunt sea creatures to the edge of extinction. The loss of large animals gains more attention, but small creatures are probably becoming extinct before we have even had time to study them.

△ This painting shows Steller's sea cows, which were hunted to extinction within 30 years of their discovery by European sailors.

The future

There is some good news. Scientific organizations such as the Intergovernmental Panel on Climate Change (IPCC) are bringing air pollution and global warming to the attention of governments. There are now more than 1,300 marine protected areas. Since 1994, the use of the oceans is governed by an international Law of the Sea treaty. As individuals, we can make a difference by not littering beaches, for example, or we can join an environmental organization. We should respect and protect our seas. Oceans are more important than we care to think. Plants in the ocean produce about half of the world's oxygen. What happens in the oceans affects our weather and climate, the food we eat, and the air we breathe. Above or below the surface, the oceans are an inexhaustible source of wonder—if we allow them to remain so.

▷ On a clean beach, the fresh air, the feel of the sand underfoot, and the sound of the surf delight people of all ages.

Endangered or extinct sea creatures	
Endangered species	**Cause**
Salmon and sturgeon	Several species of salmon and sturgeon—high-value fish that migrate between river and sea—are endangered by dam-building, overfishing, and pollution.
Seahorse	31 species of seahorse are vulnerable because of collecting. Their dried bodies are sold as souvenirs or ground up for use in Chinese traditional medicines.
Steller's sea cow	After being discovered in the Bering Sea in 1741, this 10-ton sea mammal, related to present-day dugongs and manatees, was hunted to extinction within 30 years. Its flesh was "as good as the best cuts of beef."
Northern right whale	After being heavily hunted for 800 years and protected since 1935, the population has still failed to recover. An estimated 300 to 400 survive. These slow-moving coastal whales are endangered by inbreeding, collisions with ships, and entanglement in fishing nets.
Vaquita	This very small porpoise is found only at the northern end of the Gulf of California, Mexico. Probably fewer than 500 remain. Pollution, entanglement in nets, and illegal hunting threaten their survival.
West Indian manatee	The West Indian manatee, a species of sea cow, has been reduced to a population of less than 2,000. Individuals are threatened by coastal pollution, and more than a hundred die each year following collisions with speedboats.

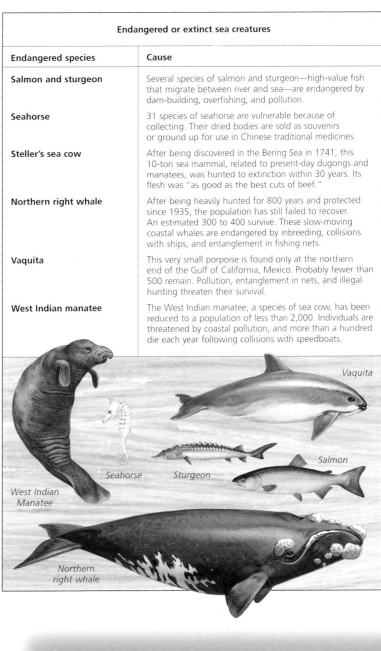

Vaquita

West Indian Manatee

Seahorse

Sturgeon

Salmon

Northern right whale

How deep can you go?

Exploring the deep

Crushingly high pressures, cold temperatures, and lack of light are major obstacles in our exploration of the deep ocean. Scuba diving is limited to depths of less than 650 feet, even with divers breathing special mixtures of gases. Hard-suited deep divers can reach 2,000 feet. Modern nuclear submarines can descend to 3,300 feet, and probably more, but some smaller underwater vehicles can dive much deeper.

Nowadays, ocean explorers prefer to use robot vehicles for deep diving. Without crew on board, the vehicles can remain at great depths for long periods without endangering human life. Astonishingly, the deepest recorded dive was achieved in 1960 when American engineer Don Walsh and Swiss explorer Jacques Piccard reached 35,800 feet in the bathyscaph *Trieste*. This strange vehicle consisted of a metal sphere slung below a float filled with gasoline.

1 Free diver: 425 feet. Lung-crushing pressures at this depth are about 13 times greater than at the surface. Free divers must train to reach such depths without injury.

2 Scuba diver using air: 475 feet. At these depths, nitrogen in the air causes nitrogen narcosis. Divers must breathe special gas mixtures beyond this depth.

3 Newtsuit: 2,000 feet. The diver is enclosed in an armor-plated suit and breathes air at surface pressure. The suit has power-assisted movable joints.

4 Bathysphere: 3,000 feet. In 1934, naturalist William Beebe and engineer Otis Barton descended in this steel ball.

5 US nuclear-powered submarine: 3,280 feet. Submarines can probably go much deeper, but the military will not say how deep.

6 Giant squid: 5,000 feet. These 60-foot long monsters are very rarely seen.

7 Giant tubeworms near Pacific hydrothermal vents: 7,300 feet. Discovered in 1977.

8 Sperm whale: 7,875 feet. These deep-diving mammals store oxygen in their muscles.

9 RMS *Titanic* wreck: 12,500 feet. The *Titanic* sank in 1912 with the loss of over 1,500 lives.

10 *Alvin* 3-person submersible: 14,750 feet. Various versions of this US submersible have been in operation since 1965.

11 AUV Autonomous Benthic Explorer (ABE): 20,000 feet. It can operate automatically over a period of several months taking photographs and collecting water and seabed samples.

12 ROV *Jason*: 20,000 feet. This vehicle operates from (and is attached to) a second ROV, *Medea*.

13 *Nautile* 3-person submersible: 20,000 feet. This French sub starred in the film *Titanic*.

14 Deepwater clams near hydrothermal vents off Japan: 20,670 feet. These clams obtain their food from bacteria which they grow specifically for this purpose.

15 *Shinkai* 3-person submersible: 20,670 feet. This is the world's deepest-diving manned submersible. In 1991, a *Shinkai* mission discovered deep-sea hydrothermal vents at a depth of 20,670 feet. These supported populations of clams and other creatures.

16 Angler fish: 27,230 feet. The deepest recorded fish.

17 ROV *Kaiko*: 35,797 feet. In 1995, this robot vehicle explored the Challenger Deep Trench within the Mariana Trench, in the Pacific Ocean.

18 Bathyscaph, *Trieste*: 35,800 feet. The Swiss Jacques Piccard and American Don Walsh made their record-breaking dive to the Challenger Deep in 1960.

19 Shrimplike amphipods live on the seafloor in the deepest parts of the ocean. Probably many other creatures live there, too.

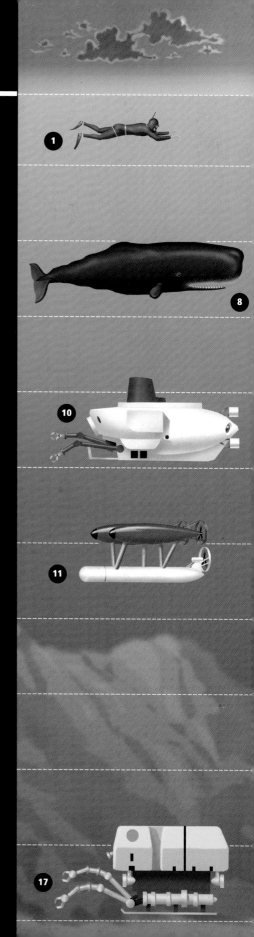

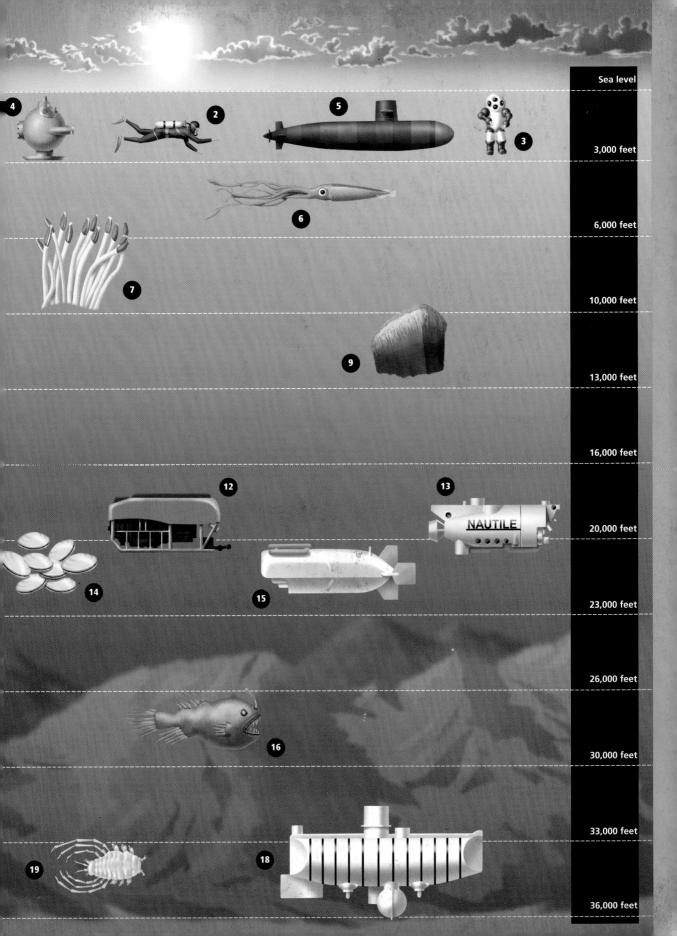

Sea level

3,000 feet

6,000 feet

10,000 feet

13,000 feet

16,000 feet

20,000 feet

23,000 feet

26,000 feet

30,000 feet

33,000 feet

36,000 feet

NAUTILE

Timeline of surface exploration

DATE	EVENT

B.C.

6000 Egyptians are using papyrus reed boats in the Mediterranean.

***c.*2500** Egyptian expeditions are traveling down the Red Sea to Punt (present-day Somalia).

***c.*2500** Sea trade between the Persian Gulf and India is well established.

***c.*1500** Polynesians and other southwest Pacific seafarers have learned to navigate beyond sight of land.

***c.*1200** The Phoenicians develop both merchant and warship galleys. Most voyages are within sight of land.

***c.*600** A Phoenician expedition under orders of the Egyptian pharaoh Necho II sails right around Africa, traveling from the Red Sea to the Mediterranean.

***c.*550** The Phoenician explorer Hanno sails from the Mediterranean down the coast of northwest Africa as far as the Gulf of Guinea.

***c.*330** The Greek explorer Pytheas sails from Massilia (present-day Marseilles) to England and Ireland.

***c.*325** The Carthaginian general Nearchus commands a fleet that sails from India to the Persian Gulf. It is the first such voyage across the Indian Ocean by Europeans.

***c.*280** The Pharos of Alexandria, Egypt, a lighthouse standing about 440 feet tall, is built. It is one of the seven wonders of the ancient world.

***c.*220** The Greek Eratosthenes publishes a chart of the known world that includes latitudinal and longitudinal lines.

DATE	EVENT

A.D.

***c.*150** The Greek-born Egyptian geographer Ptolemy compiles a map of the Earth divided into degrees of latitude and longitude.

300– 800 The Polynesians explore eastward across the Pacific Ocean, reaching New Zealand, Hawaii, and Easter Island.

***c.*982** Norse chieftain Eric the Red sails west from Iceland and discovers Greenland.

***c.*1000** Leif Ericsson sails west from Greenland to Newfoundland. He is probably the first European to discover the New World since prehistoric times.

***c.*1000** The Chinese are using a magnetic compass for navigation at sea.

1292– 1294 Marco Polo sails in a small fleet from China to the Persian Gulf, stopping at Sumatra, Sri Lanka, and India on the journey.

1325– 1348 Arab explorer Ibn Battuta crisscrosses the Red Sea, Persian Gulf, Black Sea, and the northern Indian Ocean on his many travels.

Mid- 13thC Graduated (split into 32 points) compass in use in Europe and the Middle East.

Late- 13thC Portulans (harbor-finding charts) are in use and incorporate bearings (measures of direction) to known landmarks.

1405– 1433 Chinese Admiral Zheng Ho and his fleet of junks travel widely across the northern Indian Ocean as far as East Africa.

***c.*1420** Portuguese Prince Henry the Navigator founds his famous school for navigators.

Mid- 15thC The cross staff and back staff are being used to measure latitude.

Late- 15thC The astrolabe is developed, a better instrument for calculating latitude by measuring the precise height of the Sun and stars above the horizon.

1487– 1488 Portuguese navigator Bartholomeu Dias sails around the Cape of Good Hope, the southern tip of Africa, and enters the Indian Ocean.

1492 Portuguese explorer Christopher Columbus crosses the Atlantic, from Spain to the Bahamas, and discovers the "New World" of the Americas.

1497– 1498 Portuguese explorer Vasco da Gama sails around Africa to India, opening up a new trade route.

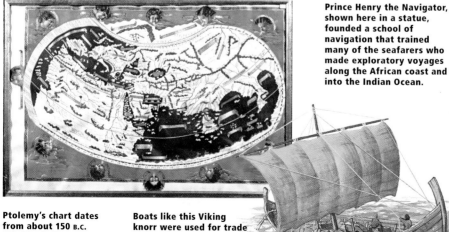

Ptolemy's chart dates from about 150 B.C. It is highly inaccurate by today's standards. It shows no sea route south of Africa.

Boats like this Viking knorr were used for trade and exploration. They sailed as far as North America in the west and Russia in the east.

Prince Henry the Navigator, shown here in a statue, founded a school of navigation that trained many of the seafarers who made exploratory voyages along the African coast and into the Indian Ocean.

1519– Portuguese nobleman.
1522 Ferdinand Magellan heads an expedition that sails right around the world. Magellan is killed in 1521, and Sebastian del Cano completes the voyage.

1530s French navigator Jacques Cartier explores the Gulf of St. Lawrence and St. Lawrence River, Canada, in his search for the Northwest Passage between the Atlantic and Pacific oceans.

1569 Cartographer Gerardus Mercator publishes the "Mercator" projection, which depicts the world globe on a flat surface.

1609 English navigator Henry Hudson explores the Hudson River and the Hudson Bay in his search for the Northwest Passage.

1675 The Royal Observatory is established at Greenwich, London, and its zero line of longitude (the Greenwich Meridian) is adopted by Britain and some other countries.

1737 Englishman John Harrison completes his first highly accurate ship's chronometer. His designs will revolutionize the accurate measurement of longitude at sea.

1769– Benjamin Franklin publishes
1770 the first ocean charts of the Gulf Stream to aid ships' captains in their passage across the North Atlantic.

1768– James Cook undertakes
1779 his three major exploratory voyages across the Pacific Ocean. He is killed by Hawaiians in 1779.

Late Sextant developed for
18thC accurately measuring the altitude (height above the horizon) of the Sun and stars for latitude and longitude measurements.

1838 The paddle-driven steamship *Sirius* crosses the Atlantic.

1872– The *Challenger* expedition
1876 led by British scientist Sir Charles Wyville Thomson is the world's first large-scale oceanographic investigation.

1884 Zero line of longitude (the Greenwich Meridian) is adopted worldwide, and henceforth international time is measured relative to it.

1893– Norwegian oceanographer
1896 Fridtjof Nansen plots the flow of pack ice across the Arctic Circle.

1895– American Joshua Slocum
1898 becomes the first person to sail around the world single-handed, in his boat, *Spray*.

1901 Italian Guglielmo Marconi sends radio signals across the Atlantic Ocean.

1903 German scientist Herman Anschutz-Kaempfer patents a design of gyroscopic compass, a device that could be set to true north rather than magnetic north.

1903– Norwegian explorer Roald
1906 Amundsen is the first to successfully navigate the Northwest Passage between the Atlantic and Pacific oceans. This ends a 300-year search for this elusive route.

1910 Frenchman Henri Fabre invents the seaplane, an aircraft that can take off and land on water.

c.1917 French physicist Paul Langevin develops an early form of echo-sounder, a device for detecting submerged objects using sound. By World War II these systems are perfected for detecting submarines and are called sonar (**SO**und **N**avigation **A**nd **R**anging).

1935 Scottish engineer Sir Robert Watson-Watt develops an aircraft-detecting radar system. Similar systems for use by ships at sea are available by the early 1940s.

1947 Norwegian Thor Heyerdahl and his crew travel across the Pacific in the balsa-wood raft *Kon-Tiki*, to try to prove that early Polynesians could have made such a voyage.

1947 The US system Loran (**LO**ng **R**ange **A**ir **N**avigation) and the British Decca Navigator enter service as electronic navigation systems. They are used on ships as well as aircraft.

1959 The first working hovercraft is tested. It crosses the English Channel in two hours.

1970 Thor Heyerdahl and his crew sail across the Atlantic in the papyrus-reed boat *Ra II*.

1978 The first remote-sensing oceanographic satellite (Seasat-A) is launched to study the ocean.

1993 The 24th Navstar satellite is placed in orbit, completing the global positioning system (GPS) that will allow anyone to establish his or her precise latitude and longitude using an inexpensive GPS device.

2000 The Argo project begins. This system of 3,000 sensory buoys will monitor the temperature, salinity, and currents of the oceans.

The astrolabe's arm was pointed toward the Sun at midday. The angle of the Sun above the horizon was used to calculate latitude.

The picture shows Columbus landing on San Salvador. He opened up the Americas to colonization by Portuguese, Spanish, and other Europeans.

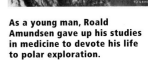

As a young man, Roald Amundsen gave up his studies in medicine to devote his life to polar exploration.

Timeline of underwater exploration

DATE	EVENT
B.C.	
*c.*4500	Mesopotamian divers are collecting shellfish from over 30-foot depths.
4thC	Aristotle describes a form of diving bell plus metal tubing used for snorkels.

DATE	EVENT
A.D.	
1545	*Mary Rose*, King Henry VIII of England's flagship, sinks near Plymouth without firing at her French enemy fleet.
*c.*1690	English scientist Edmund Halley designs and successfully tests a diving bell that is used to recover objects from wrecks.
1775	American David Bushnell invents a one-person wooden submarine, the *Turtle*. In 1776 it was used to try to sink an English ship.

1817–1818	Englishman John Ross, using a dredge, discovers life at a depth of 1.1 miles in the Arctic Ocean.
1837	German inventor Augustus Siebe tests the helmet-and-suit combination that will become the standard deep-diving gear of the 1800s.
1839–1843	Scientists on board James Clark Ross's (John Ross's nephew's) vessels dredge up sealife (starfish and worms) from a depth of about 4¼ miles in the Southern Ocean.
1855	U.S. naval officer Matthew Fontaine Maury publishes the first ocean-basin chart. Depicting the North Atlantic ocean floor, the chart was based on soundings made with a lead and line.
1858	The first transatlantic under-sea telegraph cable is laid.
1872	The world's first marine laboratory is established in Naples, Italy, by German biologist Anton Dohrn.
1872–1876	British scientist Sir Charles Wyville Thomson leads the *Challenger* expedition. This is the first true long-term scientific investigation of the world's oceans, during which many soundings and other physical measurements are taken and numerous deep-water biological samples are collected.
1908	The Scripps Institution of Oceanography is established at La Jolla, California.
1912	RMS *Titanic* sinks, with the loss of more than 1,500 lives, when it hits an iceberg.
1920	Alexander Behm bounces sound waves off the bottom of the North Sea, an early test in the development of echo-sounding, or sonar.
1925–1927	A German expedition aboard the ship *Meteor* makes detailed oceanographic studies of the Atlantic Ocean, including the use of sonar to map the ocean floor.
1930	The Woods Hole Oceanographic Institution is established at Cape Cod, Massachusetts, by Swiss zoologist Louis Agassiz.
1934	Naturalist William Beebe and engineer Otis Barton descend to a depth of 3,028 feet in a bathysphere and are the first people to directly observe deep-sea life.
1943	Frenchmen Jacques Cousteau and Emile Gagnan invent the aqualung, a form of scuba (**S**elf-**C**ontained **U**nderwater **B**reathing **A**pparatus).
1948	Swiss engineer Auguste Piccard builds the bathyscaph.
1951	Using sonar, the British ship *Challenger II* concludes that the deepest part of the ocean, the Challenger Deep, is 6.8 miles below sea level.

The *Turtle*, an egg-shaped wooden submarine, was propelled by a hand-cranked screw.

In 1934, Otis Barton and William Beebe descended to a depth of 3,028 feet in this bathysphere. They were the first to observe deep-sea life in its natural environment.

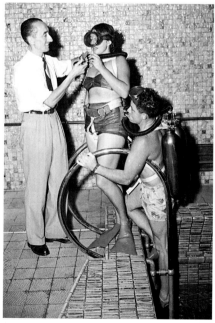

Jacques Cousteau shows young divers how to use his newly designed aqualung.

1958 The nuclear-powered USS *Nautilus* becomes the first submarine to pass under the Arctic ice cap.

1960 Jacques Piccard, Auguste Piccard's son, and American Don Walsh dive to 35,800 feet in the bathyscaph *Trieste*. This deep-diving record still stands.

1960 The nuclear-powered USS *Triton* becomes the first submarine to journey right around the world.

1962 Two men remain underwater for seven days at a depth of about 30 feet in Jacques Cousteau's *Conshelf 1* underwater shelter – a base for saturation diving.

1967 The wreck site of the *Mary Rose* is located using side-scan sonar.

1977 Scientists on board the submersible *Alvin* discover unusual life forms around deep-sea hydrothermal vents in the Pacific Ocean.

1985 Robert Ballard and an American-French team discover the wreck of the RMS *Titanic* at nearly 2½ miles depth using remotely operated vehicles (ROVs). The following year Ballard's team explores the wreck using the submersible *Alvin* connected to the ROV *Jason Junior*.

1995 The Japanese ROV *Kaiko*, reaching a depth of 35,797 feet, almost equals *Trieste*'s deep-diving record.

1995 The U.S. Navy releases satellite altimetry data. This enables geophysicists and geographers to begin compiling a detailed 3-D digital map of the world's ocean floor.

2000 The underwater laboratory Aquarius-2000 continues its program of research on coral ecology.

The WASP suit is so-named because its wearer looks like a giant wasp. A diver can descend to several hundred feet in it.

Auguste Piccard's second bathyscaph, the *Trieste II*, had a hull that contained gasoline to control the craft's buoyancy. The observation chamber slung below the hull was similar to the bathysphere.

The Swedish warship *Vasa* sank in Stockholm harbor in 1628. Salvage operations to recover the ship started in 1959. Because of the low salinity of the Baltic waters, most of the hull was intact. The ship is now preserved.

Who's who

Hanno (6th century B.C.)

Phoenician explorer. According to Hanno's account, he sailed from the Mediterranean into the Atlantic and turned south to explore the northwest African coastline probably as far as the Gulf of Guinea.

Pytheas (c.380–300 B.C.)

Greek explorer and trader. Pytheas sailed from the Mediterranean to England and Ireland, and established trade with England's tin merchants.

Eric the Red (c.950–1001)

Viking chieftain and explorer. After being banished first from Norway and then Iceland, in 982 he sailed his small fleet west and discovered Greenland. He returned to Greenland in 986 to establish a settlement there.

Leif Ericsson (c.980–1020)

Son of Eric the Red. Around 1000 this Viking seafarer became the first recorded European to reach North America in ancient times. His expedition sailed from Greenland and established a short-lived settlement on Newfoundland.

Marco Polo (1254–1324)

Medieval Italian traveler and diplomat. Marco Polo served as an adviser for 17 years to Kublai Khan, the Mongol emperor of China. In 1292–94, Polo sailed in a small fleet from China to the Persian Gulf stopping at Sumatra, Sri Lanka, and India on the way.

Ibn Battuta (1303–1365)

Tunisian-born Arab explorer. He traveled widely through Africa, Asia, and southern Europe, and crisscrossed the Red Sea, Persian Gulf, Black Sea, and parts of the Indian Ocean. His journeys were recorded in his book, the *Rihlah*.

Admiral Zheng Ho (c.1371–1434)

Chinese commander. Between 1405 and 1433 Zheng Ho's fleet explored much of the northern Indian Ocean. He set up trade and diplomatic links with many countries, from East Africa to Indonesia.

Prince Henry the Navigator (1394–1460)

Portuguese sponsor of several expeditions that charted the west coast of Africa. He founded a famous school for navigators.

Christopher Columbus (1451–1506)

Portuguese explorer sponsored by King Ferdinand and Queen Isabella of Spain. In recent historical times, he was the first European to cross the Atlantic and chart the waters of the Caribbean Islands and Central and South America.

Bartholomeu Dias (c.1450–1500)

Portuguese navigator and the first European in post-medieval times to chart the Cape of Good Hope (southern tip of Africa) and open up the way for others to sail to India and the East Indies.

Vasco da Gama (1460–1524)

Portuguese seafarer who sailed east from the Cape of Good Hope and was the European discoverer of sea routes to India and the East Indies.

Ferdinand Magellan (1480–1521)

Portuguese explorer who led the first expedition to sail right around the world. He was killed in the Philippines in 1521 before he could complete the voyage. Sebastian del Cano led the final stage of the expedition.

John Harrison (1693–1776)

Between 1730 and 1770 this Englishman built five designs of chronometer (accurate timepieces for use at sea). They revolutionized the ability of seafarers to readily determine longitude at sea.

James Cook (1728–1779)

English naval officer, explorer, and surveyor. Between 1768 and 1779 he made three long voyages that charted much of the northern, southern, central, and eastern Pacific Ocean. He was one of the first to use a marine chronometer to accurately measure longitude at sea. He was killed by Hawaiians in 1779.

Matthew Fontaine Maury (1806–1873)

American naval officer. He encouraged cooperation between scientists and mariners from different countries and has been called "the father of oceanography." In 1855, he published one of the first textbooks on oceanography: *The Physical Geography of the Sea*.

Yuly Mikhaylovich Shokalsky (1856–1940)

Russian oceanographer and geographer. Among his many achievements, Shokalsky organized the first major oceanographic explorations of the Black Sea and the Arctic seas of Russia.

Fridtjof Nansen (1861–1930)

Norwegian explorer and oceanographer. In 1893, he deliberately allowed his ship to become locked in pack ice in order to study the drift of ice across the Arctic Circle. His ship, the *Fram*, remained icebound for three years.

Roald Amundsen (1872–1928)

Norwegian polar explorer. In 1906, he became the first seafarer to successfully navigate the treacherous Northwest Passage between the Atlantic and Pacific Oceans. The voyage took three years (1903–6), with the ship locked in ice for much of the time.

William Beebe (1877–1962)

American naturalist and explorer. In 1934, he made a record-breaking descent to 3,028 feet in a bathysphere.

Auguste Piccard (1884–1962)

Swiss engineer. In 1948, Piccard developed the bathyscaph ("deep boat"). Modified versions of the design broke deep-diving records.

Thor Heyerdahl (b. 1914)

Norwegian explorer and archaeologist. Heyerdahl gained international recognition for his sea voyages, which attempted to show how ancient or historical peoples might have traveled from one continent to another. In 1947, he led his *Kon-Tiki* expedition across the Pacific in a balsa-wood raft. In 1970, his *Ra II* expedition traversed the Atlantic in a papyrus-reed boat.

Jacques Piccard (b. 1922)

Swiss undersea explorer and son of Auguste Piccard. In 1960, he descended with American engineer Don Walsh to 35,800 feet in the bathyscaph *Trieste*. This remains the deepest dive by any form of underwater vehicle.

Sylvia A. Earle (b. 1935)

American oceanographer and deep-sea diver. Earle was one of the first marine biologists to use scuba gear in scientific investigations. She has co-designed submersibles, set a deep-diving record wearing an untethered hard suit, and, in the early 1990s, served as Chief Scientist of the National Oceanographic and Atmospheric Administration (NOAA) in the U.S.A.

Robert D. Ballard (b. 1942)

American oceanographer who has pioneered the use of submersibles for exploring the ocean floor. In 1977, Ballard and John Corliss discovered hydrothermal vents 1½ miles deep in the Pacific. In 1985, his team discovered the wreck of RMS *Titanic*. In the late 1990s, they were exploring wrecks in the Black and Mediterranean seas.

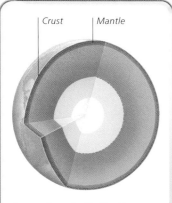

Crust | Mantle

Crust and mantle. The Earth's crust and upper mantle are made up of a dozen or so plates that float on the hot molten mantle below.

Crab

Krill

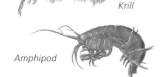

Amphipod

Crustaceans. These shelled animals vary in size from tiny plankton to large crabs. Krill are among the most abundant animals in the sea.

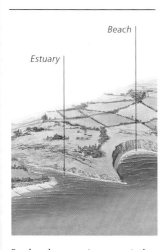

Beach

Estuary

Beach and estuary. An estuary is the widening channel of a river where it merges with the sea. Beaches form where sediment settles in sheltered parts of the coastline.

Glossary

abyssal plain The flat area of an ocean basin between the mid-ocean ridge and the continental slope.

algae Simple plant forms, such as seaweeds and plant plankton (phytoplankton). Algae lack the true roots, stems, and leaves of complex land plants.

Antarctic The cold region south of the Antarctic Circle. It includes the continent of Antarctica and part of the Southern Ocean.

aquaculture The farming of aquatic organisms such as fish, shellfish, and seaweed.

Arctic The cold region north of the Arctic Circle. It includes the North Polar pack ice, most of the Arctic Ocean, and the most northerly parts of Eurasia and North America.

atoll A ring of coral reef growing on the submerged rim of a volcanic island. It encloses a coral lagoon.

autonomous underwater vehicle (AUV) An underwater robot vehicle that can operate on its own. The latest generation of AUVs are run by sophisticated computer technology.

barrier reef A coral reef lying parallel to the shore and separated from it by a strip of water. Australia's Great Barrier Reef, at 1,180 miles long, is the world's largest barrier reef system.

bathyscaph A deep-diving vehicle consisting of a gasoline-filled float below which hangs a metal spherical cabin.

bathysphere A strong spherical steel deep-sea diving vessel. It is lowered on the end of a cable.

beach The region of the shore where loose material (such as sand, rocks and pebbles, and mud) is deposited. It extends from the lowest low tide level to the highest parts of the shore reached only by storm waves.

bends A medical condition. Dizziness and pain, and damage to joints, caused by a sudden drop in air pressure when diving. This happens when a diver surfaces too quickly and gas, particularly nitrogen, bubbles out of the bloodstream.

bioluminescence The production of light by living organisms.

buoy A float anchored to the seabed. Most buoys are navigation markers.

comet Leftover debris of ice mixed with rock from the birth of the solar system. A comet travels through near space and has a long luminous tail.

continental rise The gentle slope at the base of a continental slope. It is formed by the accumulation of sediment.

continental shelf The gently sloping edge of a continental landmass. It is submerged below shallow seawater.

continental slope The slope at the outer edge of a continental shelf.

coral polyp The individual animal in a colony of hard or soft coral. It feeds on plankton using its ring of tentacles. In hard coral, a polyp contains algae called zooxanthellae. Hard coral polyps produce a chalky skeleton that forms part of the reef.

coral reef The rocky structure that is formed from the countless billions of chalky skeletons that are laid down by hard corals.

crust The outer rocky layer of the Earth on which the land and sea lie. The crust under a continental landmass is often about 25 miles thick, whereas the crust under an ocean is typically only 3 miles thick.

crustacean An invertebrate with jointed limbs and a hard, chalky body covering. Crabs, lobsters, shrimps, copepods, and amphipods are some examples of crustaceans.

current Flowing water in the sea. An ocean current is a large mass of water that travels long distances. The Gulf Stream is an ocean current.

decompression The drop in pressure a diver encounters when returning to the surface. Slow decompression is necessary to prevent a diver from experiencing the bends.

demersal Referring to animals, particularly fish, that live on or near the bottom of the sea.

downwelling A region of the ocean where warm surface water sinks to the depths. In shallow tropical and subtropical waters, coral reefs often occur where there are downwellings.

estuary A partially enclosed area, such as the mouth of a river, where freshwater mixes with seawater.

fathom A measure of depth in the ocean. One fathom is equal to 6 feet.

food chain The chain of feeding links between different creatures in a community. In most open-ocean food chains, zooplankton feed on phytoplankton and are then eaten by larger marine animals.

fringing reef A coral reef that forms around the shore of an island, or along the coastline of a continent, and gradually extends out into the sea.

global positioning system (GPS) A system of 24 satellites that send out time and identification radio signals. An electronic GPS device picks up the signals from four or more satellites and automatically calculates the precise position on the Earth's surface.

groyne A barrier (wall or jetty) extending from the shore into the sea. It is built to block the movement of sediment along the shoreline. It helps retain particles on the beach and controls erosion of the shore.

gulf Another word for "sea," used to refer to part of an ocean, e.g. Gulf of Guinea, or to a large area of seawater connected to an ocean, e.g. Persian Gulf.

guyot A flat-topped seamount.

gyre A circular movement of surface water in the major ocean basins. Gyres rotate in a clockwise direction in the northern hemisphere and in a counterclockwise direction in the southern hemisphere.

hurricane A tropical Atlantic storm with wind speeds of 75 miles an hour or more. Similar storms in the Pacific Ocean are called typhoons, and in the Indian Ocean they are called cyclones.

hydrothermal vent A crack in the ocean floor where water, heated by the underlying rock, is forced out. Such vents are usually found at mid-ocean ridges.

iceberg A floating block of ice that has been shed (calved) from a glacier or has been broken off an ice sheet.

invertebrate An animal without a backbone (vertebral column).

knot A measure of speed used at sea. One knot equals 1.15 miles per hour.

krill A small, shrimplike crustacean that forms a major part of the plankton in polar seas. It is an important food for baleen whales.

lava Molten rock that has erupted onto the Earth's surface.

latitude A measure of north–south location on the Earth. Zero degrees of latitude lies along the equator.

longitude A measure of east–west location on the Earth. Zero degrees of longitude is called the Prime Meridian and runs north–south through Greenwich in London, England.

longline fishing A fishing method that uses long fishing lines with hundreds of baited hooks attached to them.

magma Molten rock below the Earth's surface. When it erupts onto the surface, it forms lava.

mangrove Certain trees and shrubs that can live in salty water and dominate some tropical and subtropical shores.

Turbot
Angler
Demersal fish. Fish that live on or near the bottom of the sea are among the most prized fish for food.

Iceberg. Polar regions produce several thousand giant icebergs each year. Only 10–20% of an iceberg is visible above the water.

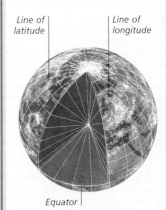
Line of latitude
Line of longitude
Equator
Latitude and longitude. Lines of longitude (meridians) run from pole to pole. Lines of latitude (parallels) circle the Earth from east to west.

Meteorite. When a large meteorite hits the Earth, it can cause immense damage. Such an impact may have caused the extinction of the dinosaurs.

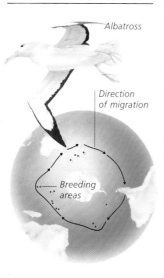

Albatross

Direction of migration

Breeding areas

Migration. After taking to the air for the first time, a young albatross may fly right around the southern oceans, feeding on the way, before arriving back at its birthplace to breed.

Octopus

Mussel

Oyster

Mollusks. These soft-bodied animals come in a wide range of shapes and sizes. Some live inside a shell; others, such as the octopus, do not have one.

mantle The layer of rock, part-molten, part-rigid, directly below the Earth's crust.

marine protected area (MPA) An area of the ocean under special legal protection that is aimed at preserving it and its creatures. Worldwide, there are more than 1,300 MPAs. The largest is the Great Barrier Reef Marine Park in Australia.

meteorite A piece of rock hurtling through near space. It journeys through Earth's atmosphere and hits the Earth's surface.

mid-ocean ridge A region of the ocean floor where the Earth's plates move apart. Here, new seafloor is created from molten rock (magma) rising from below. A typical mid-ocean ridge consists of a central rift valley (a sunken region) flanked on both sides by mountains.

migration The movement of animals from one location to another in search of food or breeding grounds.

mineral A general term for any major chemical ingredient of rock. Solids or liquids – such as coal and oil – extracted by mining are also called minerals.

mollusk A soft-bodied invertebrate such as a squid, octopus, clam, mussel, or snail.

nautical mile a unit of length equal to 115 miles.

navigation A way of determining the location of a vessel and plotting its course.

neap tide The small tidal rise and fall that occurs when the Sun and Moon are at right angles relative to the Earth.

ocean The saltwater covering 71% of the Earth. Ocean also refers to one of the four major regions of the world's ocean: the Pacific Ocean, Atlantic Ocean, Indian Ocean, or Arctic Ocean.

ocean basin A large sunken area on the Earth's surface containing an ocean.

oceanography The scientific study of the ocean and its contents.

pack ice Drifting sea ice. Pack ice is formed by the freezing of seawater, whereas icebergs originate from ice on land.

pelagic Referring to organisms that live in the surface waters or mid-waters of the ocean.

photosynthesis The process by which plants, trees, and some bacteria make their own food by trapping sunlight energy and converting it.

phytoplankton Plant plankton. They are microscopic single-celled algae. Phytoplankton include diatoms, dinoflagellates, and coccolithophores. Phytoplankton photosynthesize and, together with those bacteria (which also photosynthesize), they form the base of most food chains in the sea.

plankton Organisms that drift in the upper waters of the sea. They consist mainly of phytoplankton (plant plankton) and zooplankton (animal plankton). Most marine creatures depend upon them, directly or indirectly, for food.

plate A large rigid region of the Earth's surface. A plate is composed of the Earth's crust and the upper part of the Earth's mantle. The Earth's surface is a jigsaw of a dozen or so slowly moving plates.

plate tectonics The study of the processes by which the Earth's plates develop, move, and are destroyed.

polar Relating to the regions around the North Pole and the South Pole; the Arctic Circle and the Antarctic Circle.

predator An animal that preys upon other animals for food.

Radar (RAdio Detection And Ranging) The use of pulsed radio waves to measure the distance and direction of an object on or above the sea surface.

red tide A coloring of seawater caused by high concentrations of marine algae. Sometimes red tides are toxic (poisonous).

emotely operated vehicle (ROV) An unmanned robotic diving vehicle that is operated by remote control from a surface ship or submersible.

salinity A measure of the amount of dissolved salts, mainly sodium chloride, in seawater.

satellite remote sensing The use of satellites to detect features on the Earth's surface. Remote-sensing oceanographic satellites can detect the color, temperature, height, and roughness of the sea surface.

scuba (Self-Contained Underwater Breathing Apparatus) The aqualung is an example. Scuba divers carry their own air supply, which means they can move about freely underwater.

sea A named part of an ocean, such as Sargasso Sea. "Sea" is also used to mean the world's ocean.

seafloor spreading The process by which the Earth's plates move apart at mid-ocean ridges and new seafloor is created.

seamount An underwater volcano that rises a mile or so above the seafloor. It may remain underwater or rise above it to form an island.

sediment Particles that settle on the seafloor. They are carried by water, wind, or ice. Deep-sea sediments are mainly fine clays that may form a layer 1,650 feet thick in the oldest parts of the ocean.

shellfish Mollusks, such as clams, oysters, and mussels, which have shells. Crabs, lobsters, shrimps, and other edible crustaceans are sometimes called shellfish.

sonar (SOund Navigation And Ranging) A method for detecting objects in and on the water by sending pulses of sound and analyzing the return of their echoes.

spring tide The large rise and fall of sea level that occurs when the Sun and Moon are in alignment.

submarine canyon A steep-sided underwater valley cut into the continental shelf by a river or by underwater avalanches of water and sediment.

submersible A small, manned underwater vehicle designed for deep-sea research and observation.

tide The regular rise and fall of sea level caused by the gravitational attraction of the Moon and Sun on the Earth.

trade winds Steady winds that blow from east to west toward the equator. They arise from the surface movement of air to replace rising hot air.

transform fault A split in the ocean floor running across a mid-ocean ridge at right angles.

trawl net An open-mouthed net that is dragged through the water. It is commonly used to catch bottom-living (demersal) fish.

trench A deep trough in the ocean floor where old seafloor is taken down (subducted) into the Earth's mantle.

tsunami A gigantic, often destructive wave triggered by a volcanic eruption or underwater earthquake.

upwelling A rising to the sea surface of cold, nutrient-rich seawater from deep in the ocean.

vertebrate An animal with a backbone (vertebral column).

volcano A mound formed by molten rock (magma) erupting onto the Earth's surface as lava.

water cycle The circulation of water between land, sea, and air.

waterspout A whirling column of air at sea, similar to a tornado on land.

zooplankton Animal plankton. Zooplankton include copepods, krill, arrow worms, and the larvae (young forms) of fish and many kinds of bottom-living invertebrate. Most zooplankton feed upon phytoplankton or other zooplankton.

Mid-ocean ridge. This is a line of weakness in the Earth's crust where new seafloor is created. The new seafloor moves away from the ridge.

Plate tectonics. The dozen or so plates that form the Earth's surface are constantly moving. At their boundaries they create earthquakes and volcanoes.

Trench. Here, old seafloor is being taken down below the Earth's surface into the mantle, where it will be melted and recycled.

Lava flow

Volcano. In a volcano, molten rock from the Earth's mantle erupts as lava onto the Earth's surface. Most volcanoes rise up from the ocean floor.

Index

Acknowledgments

t = top; b = bottom; c = center; r = right; l = left

Photographic credits

1 Digital Vision; 2t Images Colour Library, 2b David B Fleetham/Oxford Scientific Films; 3tl Gianni Dagli Orti/Corbis, 3tr Raymond Blythe/Oxford Scientific Films, 3bl & br Digital Vision; 9 Aaron Horowitz/Corbis; 10t Paul Steel/The Stock Market, 10c Wolfgang Kaehler/Corbis; 13l Ric Ergenbright/Corbis, 13r Dewitt Jones/Corbis; 14 Yann Arthus-Bertrand/Corbis; 15 Douglas P Wilson – Frank Lane Picture Agency/Corbis; 16tl Wolfgang Kaehler/Corbis, 16tr M N Black/Robert Harding Picture Library, 16b Buddy Mays/Corbis; 17t Franz-Marc Frei/Corbis, 17bl Lowell Georgia/Corbis, 17br Earl Kowall/Corbis; 18t Vanderharst/Robert Harding Picture Library, 18b Roy Rainford/Robert Harding Picture Library; 19t John & Valerie Knol, 19b Douglas Peebles/Corbis; 21 Images Colour Library; 23t Peter Parks/Oxford Scientific Films, 23c Kathie Atkinson/Oxford Scientific Films, 23b Jeffrey L Rotman/Corbis; 25t Paul N Johnson/BBC Natural History Unit, 25c Jeff Foott/BBC Natural History Unit, 25b William Boyce/Corbis; 26 Jeffrey L Rotman/Corbis, 26–27 A Witte/C Mahaney/Tony Stone Images; 27t Louise Murrey/Robert Harding Picture Library, 27b Douglas Peebles/Corbis; 29t Tony Martin/Oxford Scientific Films, 29b David Samuel Robbins/Corbis; 30 Philip Gould/Corbis; 31t Roland Seitre/Still Pictures, 31c F Ruggeri/The Image Bank, 31b Ken Smith Laboratory Scripps Institute of Oceanography/Oxford Scientific Films; 32l Christian Lagereek/Tony Stone Images, 32r Aerofilms; 33t Phil Schermeister/Tony Stone Images, 33c Jim Sugar Photography/Corbis, 33b Jonathan Eastland; 34t Roland Seitre/Still Pictures, 34b Dean Conger/Corbis; 35t Roy Corral/Corbis, 35cl EPA/PA News, 35cr Ben Osbourne/Oxford Scientific Films, 35b Norbert Wu/Still Pictures; 36 Yann Arthus-Bertrand/Corbis; 37t Steve Raymer/Corbis, 37bl Danny Lehman/Corbis, 37br Corbis; 38t Kim Westerskov/Oxford Scientific Films, 38b Louis Salou/Robert Harding Picture Library; 39t Robert Harding Picture Library, 39c Peter Franks/Scripps Institute, 39b Mark Edwards/Still Pictures; 40t NGDC/NOAA, 40b Amos Nachoum/Corbis; 43 Popperfoto/Reuter; 44t Michael S Yamashita/Corbis, 44b Kim Westerskov/Oxford Scientific Films; 45 Robert Harding Picture Library; 46t Museum of the City of New York/Corbis, 46c The Stock Market/NASA, 46b Burstein Collection/Corbis; 47 Jeffrey L Rotman/Corbis; 48t(background) Lunar Planetary Institute, 48b Brandon D Cole/Corbis; 49t Rudie H Kuiter/Oxford Scientific Films, 49b Jean-Paul Ferrero/Ardea; 50t Popperfoto/Reuter, 50b The National Maritime Museum, London, 50–51 R B White; 52 (background) Bettmann/Corbis, 52 Robert Harding Picture Library; 53t Bokelberg, Werner/Image Bank, 53c & 53b Doug Allan/Oxford Scientific Films; 54l Jeffrey L Rotman/Corbis, 54r Natalie Fobes/Corbis, 55t Pat O'Hara/Corbis, 55c & 55b Natalie Fobes/Corbis; 56 Paul Simcock/Image Bank; 56-57 Roger Ressmeyer/Corbis; 57 Yogi Inc/Corbis; 58t David Paul Productions/Image Bank, 58c & 58b & 59 NOAA and UNC Wilmington; 60t Image Bank, 60b Jonathan Blair/Corbis; 60–61 Jeffrey L Rotman/Corbis; 61 & 62t Jonathan Blair/Corbis; 62b & 75 The Mary Rose Trust; 64t The Royal Lifesaving Society, 64b David H Wells/Corbis; 65t Yann Arthus-Bertrand/Corbis, 65b Digital Vision; 66tl Galen Rowell/Corbis, 66tr Chris Rainier/Corbis, 66cr Doug Allan /Oxford Scientific Films, 66bc David Vaughan/Science Photo Library; 66–67b & 67 Galen Rowell/Corbis; 68t M D /Corbis, 68c Peter Reynolds – Frank Lane Picture Agency/Corbis, 68b Galen Rowell/Corbis; 69t Stouffer Productions/Oxford Scientific Films, 69c Digital Vision, 69b Kit Kittle/Corbis; 72l Gianni Dagli Orti/Corbis, 72r Dave G Houser/Corbis; 73 Bettmann/Corbis; 74l Ralph White/Corbis, 74r Bettmann/Corbis; 75t Ralph White/Corbis, 75bl Popperfoto, 75br MacDuff Everton/Corbis; 76–77t Rick Tomlinson, 76–77b Jurgen Freund/BBC Natural History Unit.
Dividers: Overview: Images Colour Library; In Focus: David B Fleetham/Oxford Scientific; FAQs: Digital Vision; Jobfile: Raymond Blythe/Oxford Scientific Films; Factfile: Digital Vision.

Artwork credits

Allan Collinson Design 11 (cl), 53 (tr); Bernard Gudynas (Debut Art) 76–77; Chris Orr 21 (br), 22 (c), 23, 24 (b), 25 (t); Colin Newman 27, 28 (fish), 29 (tl), 69 (tc, cl, cr), 79 (t); Colin Salmon 78 (t); Colin Woolf 36–37 (b), 49, 51 (b); David Bergen 80 (t); Eric Robson 47 (tl), 58 (tr); Eugene Fleury 12 (t), 20 (c), 42 (c), 52 (b), 65, 80 (cb); Gary Hincks 11 (b), 14, 15 (t, b), 26 (br), 30 (b), 44, 79 (c); Graham Allen 69 (tl); Guy Smith 18 (b); John Francis (Bernard Thornton Artists) 47 (br), 69 (tr, b); Mainline Design 13 (c), 67 (t); Mark Franklin 41 (b), 56–57; Martin Saunders 11 (tr), 21 (tr), 29 (tr), 33 (tl), 36 (t), 45 (t), 50 (cl); Michael Welply 43; Michael Woods 25 (cr), 26 (cl), 80 (ct); Mike Foster (Maltings Partnership) 70; Oliver Burston (Debut Art) 5–8; Peter Sarson 21 (tl), 40 (bl, br), 41 (t), 42 (bl), 46 (cr), 51 (tr), 63 (b), 64, 73, 74; Richard Chasemore/Peter Sarson 19 (c); Robin Boutell (Wildlife Art) 19 (tl), 59 (b), 80 (bl); Rob Jakeway 9 (t); Roger Stewart 72, 78 (b), 79 (b), 81; Steve Kirk 58 (tl), 78 (c), 80 (bc, br); Terry Hadler (Bernard Thornton Artists) 28 (except fish).